RUSKIN
LACE & LINEN
WORK

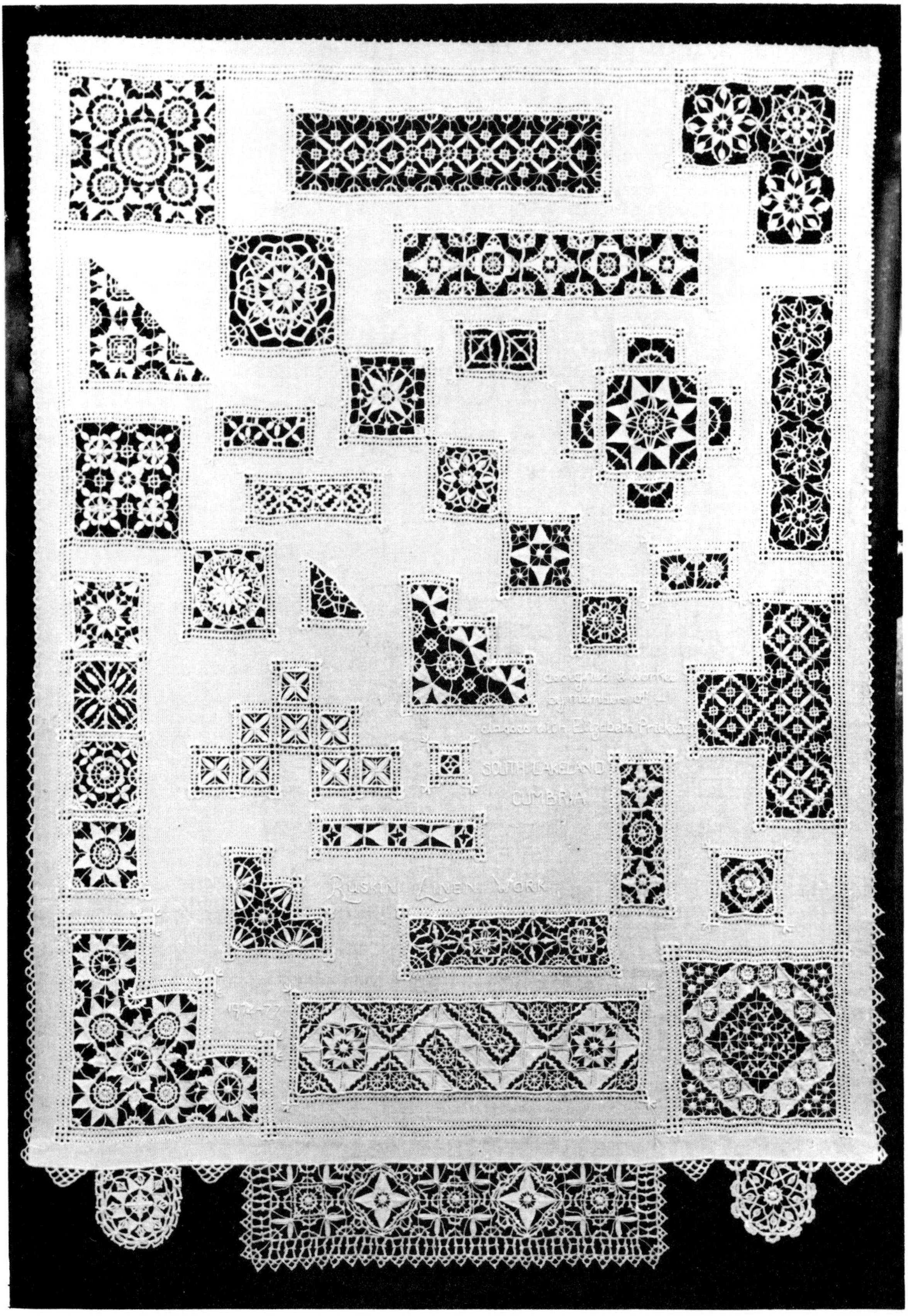
classes with Elizabeth Prickett
SOUTH LAKELAND
CUMBRIA
RUSKIN LINEN WORK

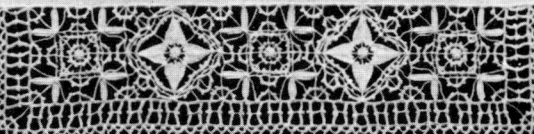

RUSKIN
LACE & LINEN
WORK

Elizabeth
Prickett

Elizabeth Prickett

Acknowledgment

I would like to acknowledge with gratitude each and every student who has attended classes and courses, without whom I would not have developed the skill and confidence to attempt to record a craft that until recent years has remained unique to the Furness and Lake District areas of England. I would like to thank in particular Mrs Lucy Jones who suggested to Mrs Winifred Raby M.B.E. that I may be capable of maintaining the standard she had spent many years establishing. A very sincere thank you to Mr L. Patch who has done the photography for this book and for the hundreds of prints he has produced over the years; also to Mr I. D. Taylor who kindly produced the colour photograph on the cover, to Greta who located the poem by John Ruskin and to Doris who researched the origin of the other verse.

Without the diligence of Mrs K. Steel, who came to live in this area, and Carolyn MacKenzie, I may not have received the invitation to write this book. Finally, a special thank you to my family for their forebearance, especially Rachel for her interest and encouragement.

Figure 1 (frontispiece) *Sampler at the Victoria and Albert Museum, London. This was a group effort involving 60 students, and took five winters to complete at Further Education classes 1972–7. It was presented to the V & A in July 1978 (Index No. T18–1979). It is worked on handspun, handwoven linen approximately 60 years old, donated by Miss Shuttleworth and Mrs J. Butterworth of Coniston, and was designed by the author.*

© Elizabeth Prickett 1985
First published 1985
Reprinted 1986
Re-issued 1997

ISBN 0 9532040 0 6

Typeset and printed by
Badger Press Ltd., Bowness-on-Windermere,
Cumbria LA23 3AS, England.
for the publisher
Elizabeth Prickett
Hollace, Torver, Coniston,
Cumbria LA21 8BH

Contents

Part II: Patterns and Edgings　51

Part III: Articles　97

Introduction

Put a pin in,
Draw a thread
Do 'four-sided'
'Til you're dead.
Petal here and picot there
Everything must fit the square.
Work a 'bug' and roll bar too,
Pyramids you all must do!
Come at two and leave at four
Back next week and do some more.
Join a class and take your place
Finish up with RUSKIN LACE!

Mrs K. White

It is now more than 100 years since the establishment of the Ruskin Linen Industry in 1883, though the production of linen ceased many years ago. One type of needlework that was originated to apply to that linen still survives, happily, today in the form of Ruskin linen or lace work. Ruskin work embraces three forms of needlework: drawn thread, cut linen and needlepoint lace. The tradition is to work directly on to the linen, producing a distinctive result with many typifying features.

This book is intended to be fully instructional and functional, in the hope that the best of the tradition will be continued and enjoyed to the full and that it will provide those who are not fortunate enough to be within the reach of tuition with the opportunity to enjoy this unique craft. I began as a young Mum looking for an absorbing interest I could pursue at home; little did I realise how this was to change the course of our lives. I now hope that my efforts will help further the creativity of those who read this book.

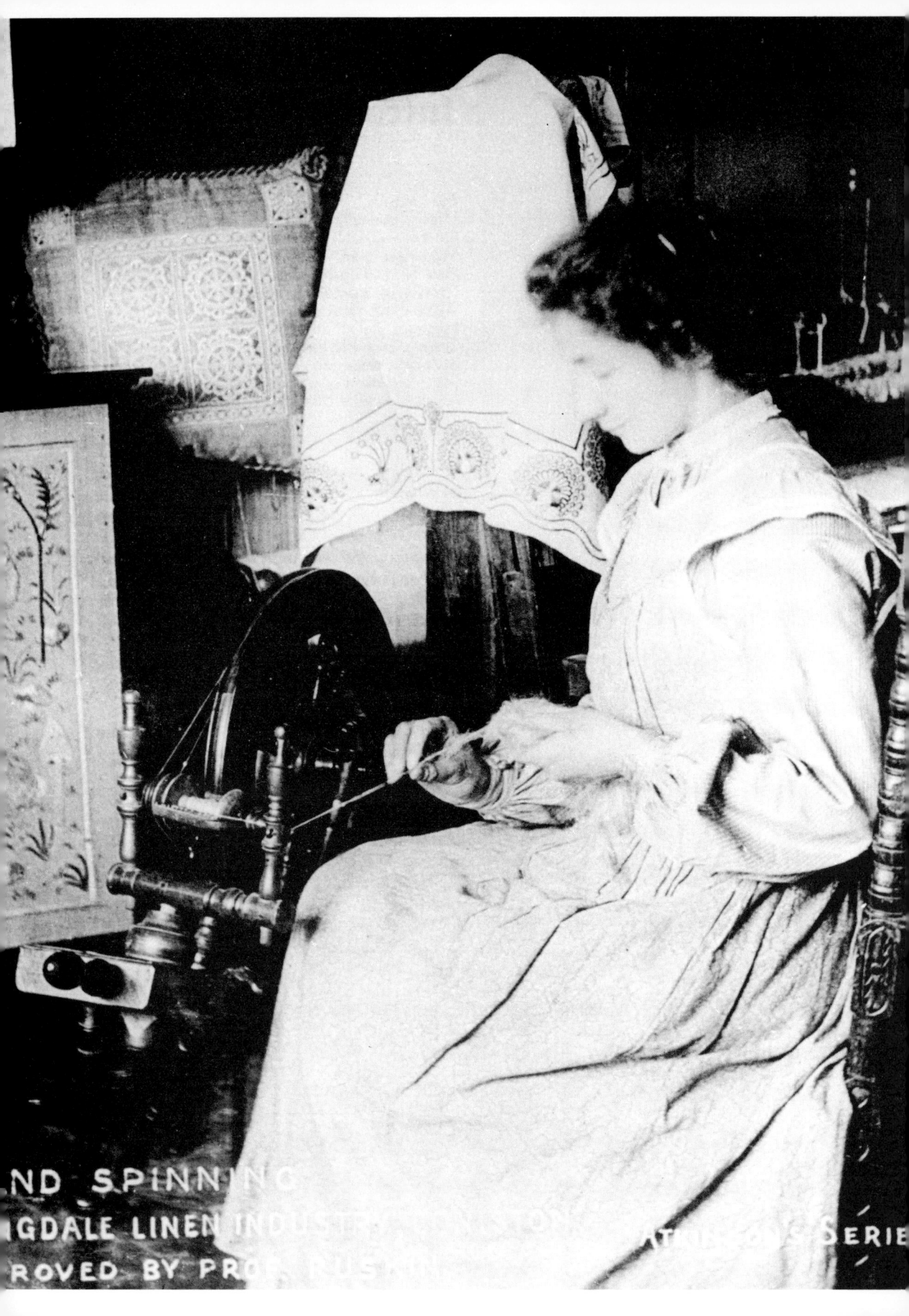

ND SPINNING
GDALE LINEN INDUSTRY
ROVED BY PROF. RUSKIN

ATKINSON'S SERIE

History

The real good of a piece of lace, then, you will find, is that it should show, first, that the designer of it had a pretty fancy; next, that the maker of it had fine fingers; lastly, that the wearer of it has worthiness or dignity enough to obtain what is difficult to obtain, and common sense enough not to wear it on all occasions.

John Ruskin

John Ruskin was instrumental in the revival of linen fabric production as a cottage industry.

This came about when he came to live at Brantwood, Coniston, in the Lake District, in 1872. He showed great concern for the well-being of the local people and the need for a pastime that could supplement their income. In some parts of the Lake District and surrounding areas in Cumbria a condition of tenancy to some of the farms was to grow and process flax into a fabric called 'harden sark'. 'Hards' are the coarse fibres of hemp or flax and 'sark' was a shirt, though not a shirt as we know it today; it was used as an outer garment.

With this in mind, John Ruskin was successful in enthusing others who were able to further this venture. One such person was Albert Fleming, who at that time lived at Neaum Crag, Skelwith Bridge, a village within six miles of Coniston. Albert Fleming and John Ruskin were both companions to the Guild of St George which had been formed to help the furtherance of country life in the best traditions of agriculture, education and handiwork.

But it is to Marion Twelves, Albert Fleming's housekeeper, that I owe the privilege of recording this history. Having managed, eventually to procure an old spinning wheel, she

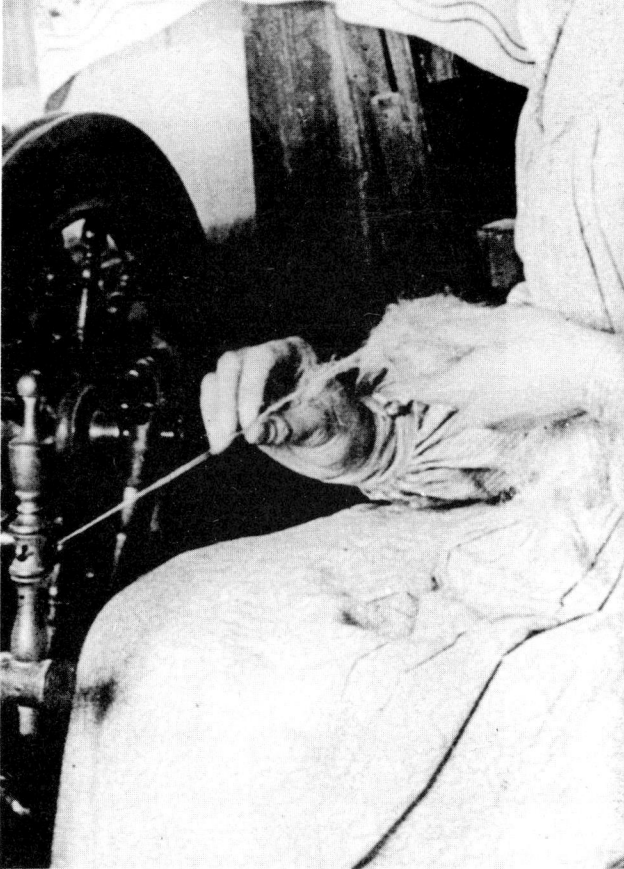

Figure 3 *The technique of spinning flax practised in the Langdale Linen Industry* (reproduced by kind permission of James Atkinson, Ulverston)

set about teaching herself to spin, with the help of an elderly local lady resident who had been taught to spin as a child. A local carpenter was then commissioned to produce more spinning wheels to the same pattern.

From here, Marion Twelves became the prime instigator. A cottage at Elterwater in the Langdale Valley was acquired by the Guild of St George and renamed 'St Martins'. Here the local women could learn to spin and, when proficient, were allowed to take a spinning wheel home. The spinsters were rewarded at the rate of 2/6 (12½p) per pound of thread. A spinning wheel bobbin would hold approximately 2 oz (56 g) of thread and some 500 yd (460 m) of the thickness that was eventually spun for the finer linens.

The need for a loom soon became evident, and this came as a gift, in pieces, from a

Figure 2 *A spinner at work: Mrs Nelson, daughter of Mrs Elizabeth Pepper, using one of the original spinning wheels* (reproduced by kind permission of James Atkinson, Ulverston)

9

HAND WEAVING.
LANGDALE LINEN INDUSTRY, CONISTON.
APPROVED BY PROF. RUSKIN.

ATKINSON

Figure 4 *Mrs Elizabeth Pepper at her loom*
(reproduced by kind permission of James
Atkinson, Ulverston)

weaver in Kendal who no longer needed it.
But no one at St Martins knew how to
assemble it until they were lent a photograph
of Giotto's 'Campanile' in Florence where the
Italian cottage weaver was depicted on a mural
in the Duomo Tower.

A retired weaver from the Kendal establishment was persuaded to live and work at St
Martins for the princely sum of 16/- (80p) per
week.

The first linen, 20 yd in length, came off the
loom at Easter 1884. Albert Fleming wrote to
John Ruskin:

> I own it seems terrible stuff, frightful in colour
> and of dreadful roughness with huge lumps and
> knots meandering up and down its surface. But
> we took heart of grace and refreshed ourselves

by reading the beautiful passage in the *Seven
Lamps*, which convinced us that these little
irregularities were really honourable badges of
all true handiwork. Better still an elect lady
called one day and even without preliminary
refreshment of the passage, she pronounced the
stuff delightful and bought a dozen yards at 4/-
(20p) per yard.'

In 1889 Marion Twelves moved to Keswick
to join Mrs Canon Rawnsley at the Keswick
Arts Industry in the hope of enjoying more
independence, leaving Mrs Elizabeth Pepper
in charge at St Martins, Elterwater. The Guild
of St George helped Marion Twelves purchase
'Porch Cottage' and, in 1894, she established
her industry of spinning and weaving linen
there as she had done at Elterwater. There she
continued to work until the 1920s, giving 35
years of her life to this end.

Before leaving Elterwater Marion Twelves

10

Figure 5 *A square mat worked by the author, using linen spun and woven by hand by Mrs Coward of Coniston. The pattern is based on a ½ in. (1.3 cm) unit which has no basic grid; the original threads are worked in double buttonhole stitch.*

had realised that if the linen was made up into garments, it would provide work for even more local women, and so she began to teach many forms of embroidery to be applied to various domestic and personal articles, demand for which seemed to be greater than supply.

One of these forms of embroidery was known as Greek lace, though this was a misnomer. In an article that Marion Twelves wrote for the magazine of the National League of Handicraft Societies in America there is reference to a class of 'Greek lace workers in Coniston village who were taught some five years since under my supervision, expenses over and above a fee of 5/- [25p] each paid by the students was defrayed by the Guild of St George'. This must have been a forerunner of further education as we know it today.

On 8 February 1894 on his birthday, John Ruskin gave Marion Twelves a signed authority to use his name and his motto 'Today' as a trademark. In the same article as above she says 'a photographed copy of which [authority] I send to be used with this article if desired, and I here set down once and for all that my industry is the only one of any description having authority from Mr Ruskin to use his name, and that no other industry in the Lake District or elsewhere has any connection with it, except a class of Greek lace workers in Coniston.'

When John Ruskin died in 1900, Marion Twelves and her workers at Keswick made a pall of natural-coloured linen to cover his coffin. It was embroidered with silk floss thread, with a central wreath of wild roses enclosing the words 'Unto this last, J.R.', with petals and leaves scattered over the surface and lined with rose pink silk. This pall is now in the Ruskin Museum, Coniston, Cumbria.

In 1907, Marion Twelves travelled to Ambleside to take a month's course of daily lessons in Greek lace, now known as Ruskin lace or Ruskin linen work, followed in 1909 by a course of ten days' duration. The latter was followed by an exhibition with names appearing in the catalogue from Grasmere, Langdale, Coniston, Windermere as well as Ambleside.

Possibly hearing of the earlier classes held in Coniston, Mrs Alan Coward of Coniston found her way to the sessions at Ambleside, along with other ladies of the area. Mrs Coward was also a proficient spinner and weaver, possibly having acquired her skill through connections with Mrs Elizabeth Pepper at Elterwater and later at Tilberthwaite.

Many ladies were involved as out-workers for Marion Twelves at Keswick, Elizabeth Pepper at Elterwater, Annie Garnett at Windermere, Mrs Coward at Coniston and Miss Butterworth at Flax Home, Grasmere, as well as others in the area, and there was plenty of demand for their work.

Mrs Coward was the sister-in-law of the schoolmaster at Broughton-in-Furness who had to organise Adult Education Classes and, in 1932 Mrs Coward was duly invited to take a class for Greek lace. Time has proved that this action secured the continuation of the craft as

we know it today. Unfortunately Mrs Coward died quite suddenly shortly before the 1934 session was due to begin.

One of Mrs Coward's pupils at Broughton-in-Furness, Mrs Winifred Raby, stepped into the breach for what she thought would be a temporary situation. Little did she realise that this temporary situation was to last for 36 years, during which time many changes were to take place.

The production of handspun, handwoven linen ceased in the late 1930s. A manufactured linen was introduced in the form of Glenshee Evenweave, a line linen we still use today, with 29 threads to the inch, as compared to the 30–36 threads to the inch of the earlier handwoven linen, and from which threads can be withdrawn easily. Thread sources and types have changed and, during the Second World War years, supplies of both linen and threads were often scarce and difficult to obtain.

Mrs Winifred Raby was able to establish classes in the Furness areas at Kirkby and Dalton, Grange-over-Sands and Broughton-in-Furness. Through the 1940s transport was difficult; it took her most of the day to travel to Grange-over-Sands from her home at Broughton-in-Furness, take the class and get home again – a return journey of approximately 50 miles. Partly for her efforts and stalwart determination to keep the craft alive and partly for her work in other organisations, she was awarded the M.B.E. when she retired in 1970.

Three winters prior to Mrs Raby's retirement, I had attended the class at Broughton-in-Furness and had become besotted with the craft. Little did I realise that the acceptance of the invitation to continue the furtherance of this craft would be so satisfying, rewarding and fulfilling.

In the face of mass-production there are still many ladies eager and happy to learn the traditional skills, producing articles that are beyond the constraints of commercial viability in which the craft had its beginning. Now, a century later, Ruskin lacemaking is going from strength to strength as a very satisfying leisure activity.

Figure 6 *Brush and comb bag. This bag was purchased in Coniston in approximately 1916. Made of handspun handwoven linen, it was worked with Silk Floss thread and lined with silk fabric.*

Part I

MATERIALS & TECHNIQUES

One of the advantages of this craft is that the equipment and materials are few. Any fabric can be used, so long as a thread can be withdrawn easily, though traditionally an evenweave linen fabric is used. The most suitable linen is Glenshee evenweave at 29 threads to the inch.

The lace-work area is mounted on to leathercloth or a rexene-type material that has a woven backing. This is to maintain the shape of the lace-work area while the inside area of linen is cut away and the lace-work pattern worked.

Linen lace thread is used whenever possible, of a weight or thickness equal to that of the fabric. For use with Glenshee Linen Barbour, Campbell's No. 50 or Bocken's No. 35 are suitable threads.

For the best results a round-eyed needle is used in the form of a Sharps or Betweens, usually a No. 6; this prevents the thread from becoming softened and fluffy. This type of needle is used throughout, except for the four-sided stitch when a tapestry needle No. 22 is used.

A thimble will be found to be invaluable – this work converted me to the use of one – a clearly marked tape-measure useful and a pair of sharp-pointed embroidery scissors essential.

Preparation of linen

A thread is withdrawn to ascertain measurement. Often linen will appear to be distorted; this is because it is baled folded. If it is cut using a drawn thread and hems are folded according to the following instructions, there will be no need to pull and tug the linen into shape.

To lay a hem

Make all measurements along the grain of one thread. Measure from the outside edge of the linen, twice the depth of the required finished

hem, plus $\frac{1}{4}$ in. (6 mm) for the first turn. For example, for $\frac{1}{2}$ in. (1.3 cm) hem, measure $1\frac{1}{4}$ in. (3.2 cm) from the outside edge and pick up on a pin the next two threads beyond the measurement.

The only exception is in the event of a $\frac{1}{4}$ in. (6 mm) hem, when we allow twice the depth of the finished hem, but only $\frac{1}{8}$ in. (3 mm) for the first turn. For example, measure $\frac{5}{8}$ in. (15 cm) from the outside edge and pick up on a pin the next two threads beyond the measurement. When locating these two threads, make sure they are picked up well away from the point where the two threads on the two adjacent sides will eventually meet. *Threads are not withdrawn completely to the outside edge.*

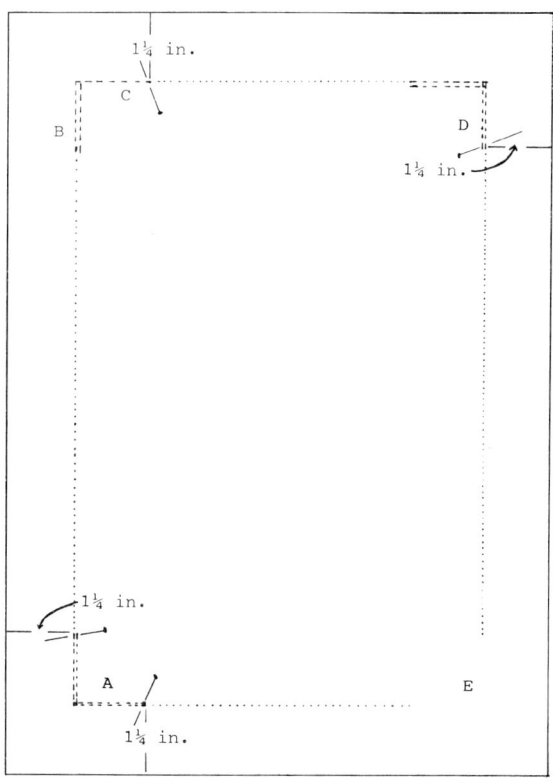

Diagram 1 *Laying a $\frac{1}{2}$ in. (1.3 cm) hem*

The most convenient order of working is to begin at one corner of the fabric, take measurements on each side of the corner well away from the point where the two pairs will meet (diagram 1 [A]).* Cut threads where picked up and unpick back to form a right angle, working clockwise, or to the left. Pull the outer thread of the two cut and trace along towards the next right angle or corner at B, pick up and cut this thread and the one innermost, well away from the next right angle, and withdraw these two threads. Turn the fabric a quarter turn to the right and make the third measurement at C, and repeat as for the previous side from *. Turn the fabric as before and measure the fourth side, at D, repeat from * to *. Draw the two threads from the right angle back to meet the threads from the fourth side at E, cutting well away from the point of merging.

Picking up threads on a pin, then checking them will help prevent cutting wrong threads and having to repair or replace them.

To repair or replace a wrongly cut or withdrawn thread

Use a Sharps needle and a length of withdrawn thread, longer than required. Unless the thread has just been withdrawn too far, it is better to use another length of thread rather than try to replace the offending end, as it is advisable to overlap the wrongly cut ends. Introduce the new thread approximately ½ in. (1.3 cm) before it is actually needed by passing the needle through the unders and overs and placing the new thread on *top* of the old one. Leave an end of thread protruding; then, weaving along the spacing in the position in which the thread is intended to remain, overlap the other end as in the beginning. Cut off the old threads and the replacement close to the fabric.

To fold a hem

Turn the fabric over, with the wrong side uppermost and lay it on a flat surface. The long sides of an oblong article are folded first or, in the case of a square, the opposite sides are folded.

Begin by folding over ¼ in. (6 mm) centrally along one side (diagram 2). By working on a

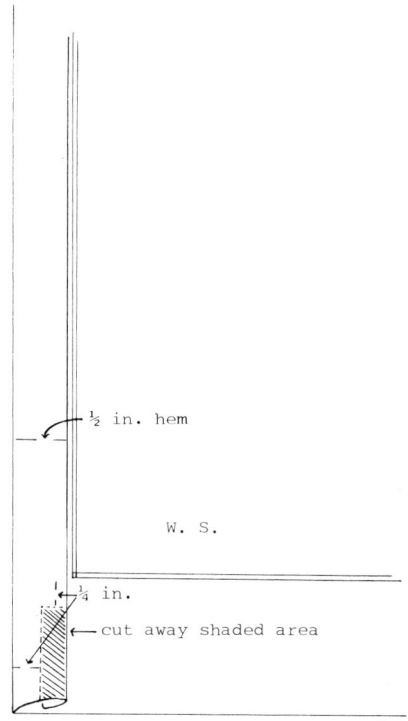

½ in. hem

W. S.

¼ in.

cut away shaded area

Diagram 2 *Folding a hem*

flat surface it will be easier to fold along the grain of one thread. Fold out to each end. Turn the fold to lie just outside the two withdrawn threads, making sure the grain is straight (this will rectify any distortion of the fabric). Square corners are a traditional feature of Ruskin work, so we need to remove excess bulk from the corners. To do this on hems of ⅜ in. (1 cm) or deeper, cut away ¼ in. (6 mm) from the outer edge, as in diagram 2, cutting back along the folded edge – this removes the first turn and part of the second fold – and stop ¼ in. (6 mm) away from the two threads withdrawn on the next side. For a ¼ in. (6 mm) hem, only the depth of the first turn is removed, otherwise the corner would be weakened. Fold the other two sides in the same way to form square corners. Tack.

Slip-stitching

If self thread can be used for the slip-stitching, which is a necessary means of securing the hem, the stitching will be least noticeable. (Self thread is that which has been withdrawn from the article or frayed from surplus fabric.) Any self thread which is two-fold, as in Glenshee linen, is perfectly adequate for this purpose; otherwise it will be necessary to substitute a thread of matching colour to the fabric.

The most successful method of slip-stitching is as follows: with the wrong side of the fabric facing, hold the hem in the left hand and prepare to work right to left. Begin the thread by passing the needle through the hem and bringing it out at the inner fold; make a small back stitch into the inner edge of the hem. Hold the needle horizontally to the hem, picking up a small amount of fabric at the inner edge of the hem then cross to the space where threads have been withdrawn. Pick up a small amount of vertical thread, as in diagram 3, in the drawn-out space and repeat frequently so as not to leave a long thread between contacts. Work a number of repeats before withdrawing the needle.

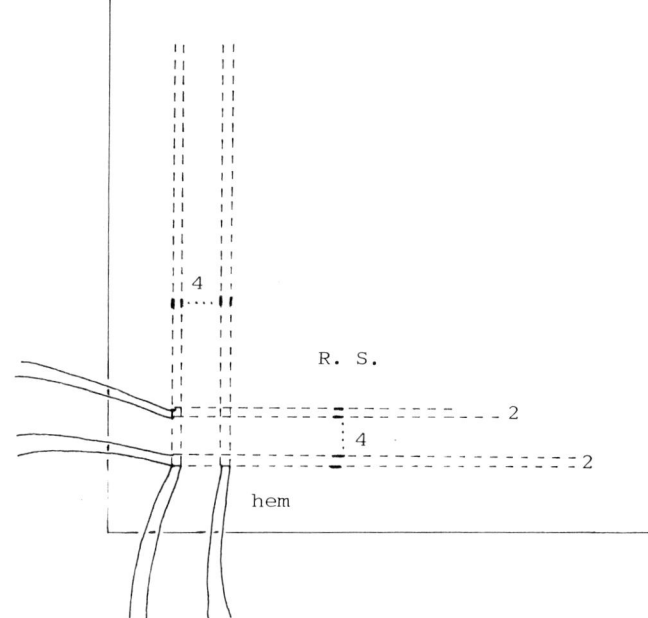

Diagram 4 *Drawing threads for four-sided stitch border*

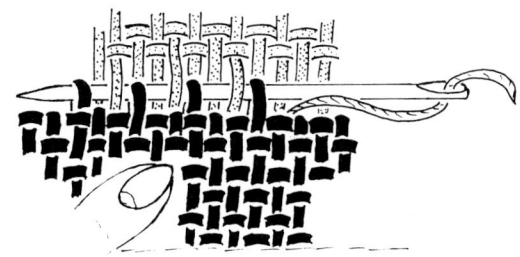

Diagram 3 *Slip-stitching a hem*

To draw threads for a four-sided stitch border

This is another typifying feature of Ruskin work (diagram 4). This stitch is always worked as a border immediately inside the hem and also surrounds the pattern areas. This stitch can be worked as a single row or in multiples.

Single four-sided stitch border
When this is worked immediately inside the hem, with the right side of the fabric uppermost, two threads have already been withdrawn to ensure a straight hem. Leave four threads, draw the next two inside threads. The second two threads are withdrawn to the outside of the initial two threads, as in diagram 4. Whenever possible, cut the threads well away from the junction of the corner; this is so that they can be held back out of the way whilst working the four-sided stitch. They will be reduced and utilised later.

Double and multiple rows of four-sided stitch
Draw threads as above, * then leave another four threads, draw two threads *. For multiple rows, repeat from * to * as required. Refer to diagram 7 (see p. 21), for a similar example.

Working four-sided stitch

Use a tapestry needle, bringing it up from underneath at A (diagram 5a). Leave an end on the under-side and lay along under the four threads being worked over, to be included. Begin in the far right-hand corner of the article or pattern area. This is so that, in case of the outer border especially, the bulk of the work will be resting on the worker's lap – life is easier that way. There are two stitches worked on each side of a block of four threads.

19

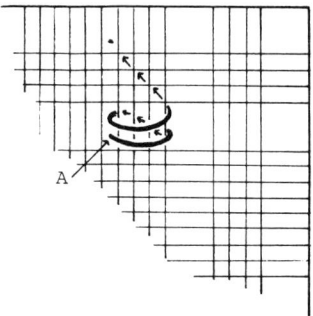

Diagram 5a *To begin four-sided stitch*

Take the needle down at B and out at A; again in at B and out diagonally underneath at C; in at D and out at C; again in at D and out diagonally down to A; in at C and out at A again; in at C again and out diagonally at E to begin another block repeating from A as in diagram 5b. Continue in this manner until the next corner is approaching. At approximately ½ in. (1.3 cm) away, count the last few threads and divide into blocks of four or three; never two or five, as the area will have been measured, therefore threads will not be in multiples of four. Take care not to pull the stitch

tight but allow the thread to wrap round the fabric threads closely without being loose. A tight ridge should not form along the border, otherwise the surrounding area or hem will be fluted and the inside area, especially over a small pattern area, will be distorted.

To finish and restart a thread
Take the needle down to the underneath at any stage of the stitch and pass it through approximately three blocks of crosses, back stitch around one thread and continue under three more blocks. Restart another length of thread reversing the previous procedure and bringing the needle up into the next position to continue.

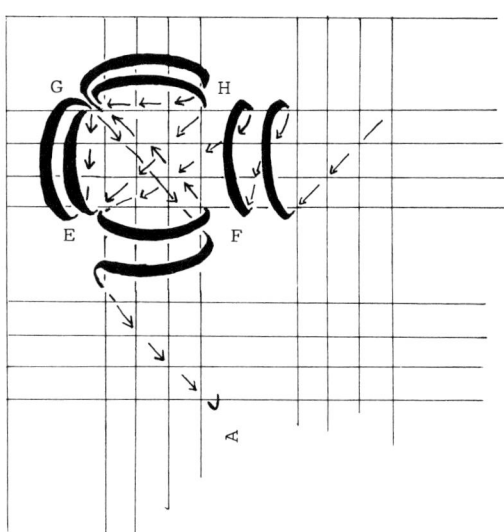

Diagram 6 *To turn a corner in four-sided stitch*

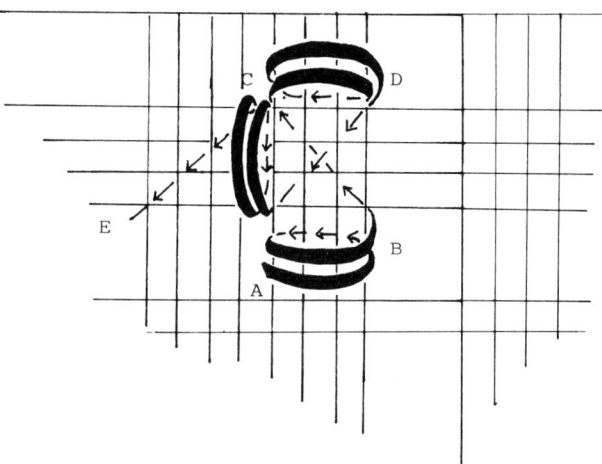

Diagram 5b *To work four-sided stitch*

To turn a corner
Work to E, then refer to diagram 6. There is only one stitch around the bottom of the block at this stage. Take the needle in at F and out diagonally at G; in at H and out at G; again in at H and out diagonally at E; turn work a quarter turn to the left so that the next side is lying horizontally; in at G and out at E; in at G and out diagonally at F; in at E, to put the second stitch over and diagonally out at A, to continue along the next side.

20

Working multiple rows of four-sided stitch

There must still be two stitches on each side of the block. To achieve this, when working the outer row make only one stitch at the bottom of the block. If only a double row of four-sided stitch is required then there will be one stitch around the top of the block on the inner row. If more than two rows are required then there will be one stitch around the top and bottom of the block on intervening rows.

It will be observed that the more rows of threads withdrawn, the more spaces appear at the corners; these can be made into a feature later. When working the four-sided stitch do not encroach into the spaces; therefore finish at D, in diagram 5b. (Refer to diagram 7.)

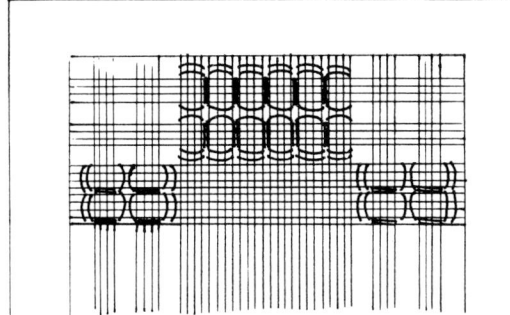

Diagram 7 *Double four-sided stitch, leaving corners unworked*

Woven corners

These are decorative features that can be worked into the spaces which appear at the corners when double or multiple rows of four-sided stitch have been worked.

Using a Sharps needle, begin by running the thread through the crosses on the side as described on page 20. Bring the needle up between one pair of the four threads and one thread back from the corner. One foundation thread needs to be added to lie on top of each pair of the original threads, as in diagram 8. Bring the needle up between the two columns of (now) three threads, * take the needle around the right-hand column and up through the middle of the two columns, take the needle to the left and up through the middle again,

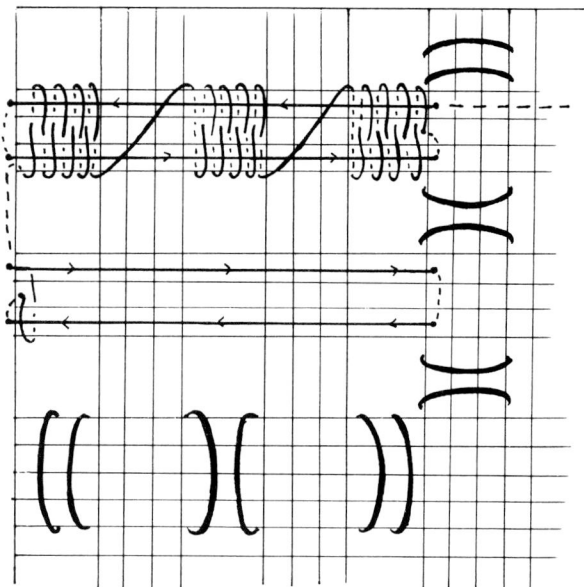

Diagram 8 *Woven corners, stage one*

repeat from * three times more. Do not be tempted to work more than four rows. After completing the fourth row, take the needle under and across to the right, pass diagonally over the junction to the left and, from underneath, bring the needle up between the two columns of three threads *. Repeat from * to *

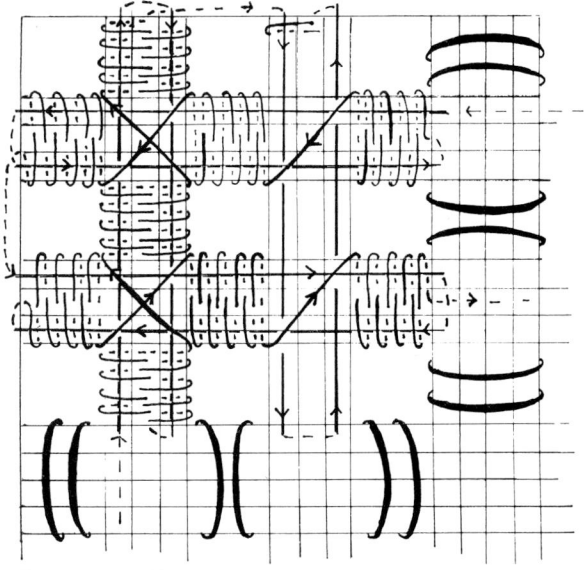

Diagram 9 *Woven corners, stage two*

as required, to end of row. If the thread in the needle is long enough to work another row, slip through the fabric close to the inside edge to lay the extra foundation threads for the next row and repeat in the exact sequence as before.

When all rows in one direction are completed repeat as above for the opposites, except that the foundation threads are passed under the half crosses which now appear over the junctions. The crosses will then be completed over the junctions, as in diagram 9. The thread is now finished off in the same way as it began.

Drawing threads for pattern areas

There are various methods of doing this depending on the shape and situation of the article. A four-sided stitch border is worked around all pattern areas. Where one begins to draw threads for a square, which can be of any size, will be determined by the size of article or its relation to the pattern layout as a whole.

Squares attached to a border

If a square is to be positioned centrally on an article then plot from the centre of the square outwards, as in diagram 10. First find the centre of the article or area. Decide on the size of square to be worked, then mark half the measurement on each side of the centre, fol-

lowing the grain of the fabric so that the measurement will stay accurate if the fabric is not completely straight. Pick up on a pin the two outermost threads at each end of the measurement, leave the next four threads and pick up the next two outermost threads. Repeat in the opposite direction. It will be noted that threads are picked up well away from the corners of the square; this needs to be practised whenever threads are to be withdrawn and will result in long ends at all corners. This makes working easier, as the long ends can be held back out of the way when working. Cut the outer two threads on all sides and draw any two adjacent sides back to the point where four threads merge, resulting in a square of two drawn-out threads. Cut the inner two threads on all sides and draw back to the outside of the outer threads, forming an isolated block of four threads in each corner. Four-sided stitch is now worked over this border.

Detached square

In this instance the square is close to another border or relative to another part of the layout. The margin between this and the square must be decided. The minimum margin should be eight threads; less than this interferes with the neatening of corners at a later stage.

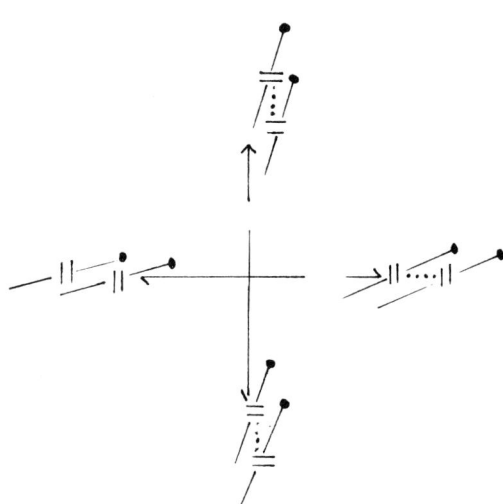

Diagram 10 *Plotting a square, from the centre*

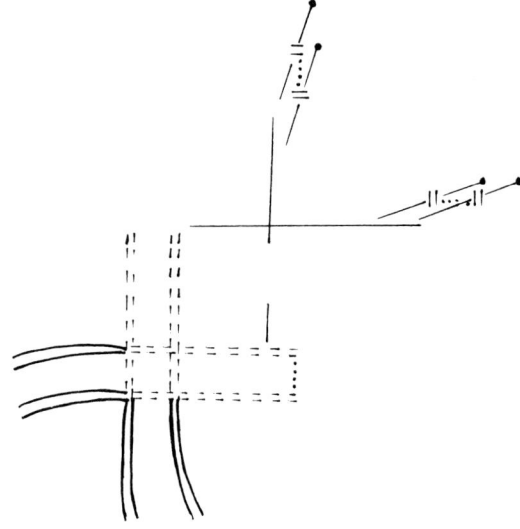

Diagram 11 *Plotting a square, from a right angle*

Once the margin has been decided, follow diagram 11. Pick up on a pin two threads well away from where the junction of the corner is expected to fall, leave four threads and pick up the next two innermost threads. Repeat on the next side to form a right angle to the side just plotted. Cut the outer two pairs of threads on each side and draw back to the point where all four threads merge. Cut the inner two pairs of threads and draw back to the outside of the previously withdrawn threads; this forms an isolated block of four threads at the corner. Measure from the innermost of the inner two threads, along the grain of the fabric or along the line of one thread, for the required pattern measurement, pick up two threads beyond the measurement, leave four threads, pick up two in both directions to complete the plotting of the square. Cut the outer two threads and draw back to meet the threads from the initial right angle, draw the other cut ends back to form the fourth right angle, thus completing the outer circuit and draw the inner cut ends back to complete the inner circuit of the square. This is now ready for four-sided stitch to be worked as described on pages 19 and 20 and in diagrams 5 and 6.

Squares can be positioned obliquely or diagonally; this positioning can be applied to tablecloths, lampshades, wall hangings and samplers. This arrangement can be repeated as required, area permitting. By referring to photographs in this book where this arrangement occurs it will be noted that two sides of the previous square automatically form two sides of the next square. The size of the squares set diagonally can vary in size as the worker desires.

Plotting the inside area of a square

Following diagram 12, leave the four threads innermost of the four-sided stitch border, pick up on a pin the next thread innermost and, horizontally to the border, at about the centre of each side of the square, cut and unpick back to the point where two cut ends from adjacent sides meet.

* Find the centre three threads of the inner area of the square. To do this, pick up on a pin

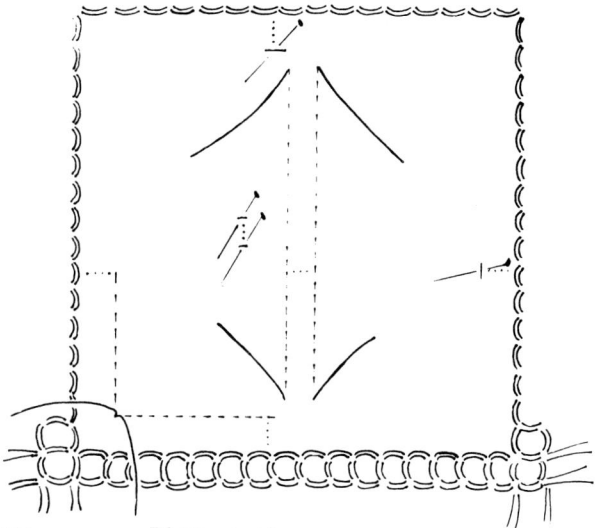

Diagram 12 *Plotting inside square area*

at random three threads centrally in one direction. Count the threads in each half of the square and adjust the three threads picked up on the pin accordingly. If it proves there is an odd thread in one half, adjust the three threads picked up so that it is least noticeable. Cut one thread in the middle on each side of the centre three threads, and unpick each cut end back towards the one previously taken out on all sides, stopping just inside this thread. Repeat from * in the opposite direction which will then form a cross of three outlined threads. These three threads are retained and used later to form part of the basic foundation.

Mounting on to leathercloth

This is to maintain the size and shape of the cut-out area, regardless of how small this area is to be, whilst working the pattern.

A piece of leathercloth larger than the intended pattern area by about 1 in. (2.5 cm) all round, is placed to the underside of the pattern area with the vinyl side uppermost to the fabric. Begin to attach the leathercloth to the fabric at a corner of the shape, using a sharp needle and strong thread, such as double tacking thread or, if working on linen, then surplus withdrawn self thread is ideal. Work a form of back stitch: instead of taking the needle back to where it came out previously, go only halfway back; in this way more con-

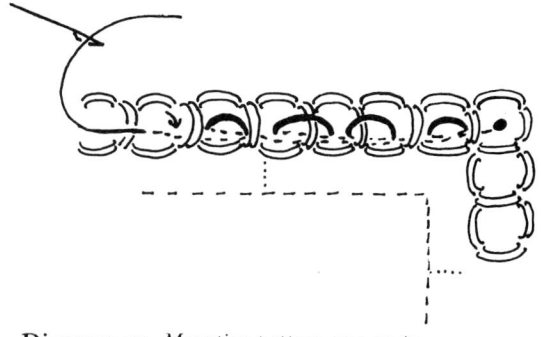

Diagram 13 *Mounting pattern area on to leathercloth, back stitch*

tacts between the two fabrics can be made to help prevent contraction of the pattern area as it is being worked. Make the stitches through the middle of the four threads used in the four-sided stitch, as in diagram 13. Stretch slightly, hold fabric taut along the length of the border stitch and pull stitches tight. Fix each side straight to form a good right angle with the previous side attached. When complete, the inner pattern area should be taut and the centre cross of three threads square. Patience will be justly rewarded in the end result; weakness here cannot be rectified once the next two stages have been worked.

When multiple or double rows of four-sided stitch have been worked, the back stitch attachment must be made along the innermost row nearest to the pattern area.

Spaced whipping

This stitch is worked over the inner margin of the four threads on the inside of the four-sided stitch. Using a Sharps needle and working

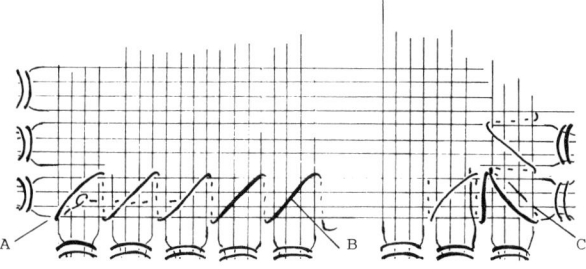

Diagram 14 *Spaced whipping*

thread, begin by running the thread into these four threads and work a back stitch (to anchor the thread) before coming out at the bottom left-hand corner, as at A (diagram 14) at the outside diagonal point of the corner, to work from left to right or anticlockwise. Take the needle diagonally over the corner to the inside junction of the four threads, out at the next space along towards the right, created by the four-sided stitch, and in above the next space along – this will usually be four threads along. There will be a left-to-right slanting stitch on the upper side of the work with a straight stitch on the under-side.

Organise the whip stitch so that the centre three threads that are to be retained are in one block or group, as in B, and that a diagonal stitch falls over each corner, as in C. This is a marker for the next stage. Continue to complete the circuit. If there is more than 6 in. (15 cm) of thread remaining in the needle, make a tiny back stitch into the four threads before bringing the needle out finally at the outside of the corner, as in the first instance. Otherwise, finish the thread off as it was begun. Rejoin thread, if need be, as before but in another corner.

Padded roll

This is worked over the four whipped threads as a close whip stitch incorporating a padding cord of three threads.

To make padding cord. With the working thread, make a generous continuous measurement of the four thread whipped border. Make the cord three times this length, knot together at one end and cut any loops there are at the other end, so that there are now three separate threads knotted together at one end.

Lay the padding cord over the four whipped threads with the knotted end extending just beyond the bottom left-hand corner, as in diagram 15. Make the first whip stitch lie diagonally over the corner: as the needle is taken underneath, pick up a small amount of fabric (with running stitch action) and pull tight. The diagonal stitches over each corner are the only stitches to be pulled up tight; all others must just wrap closely without being

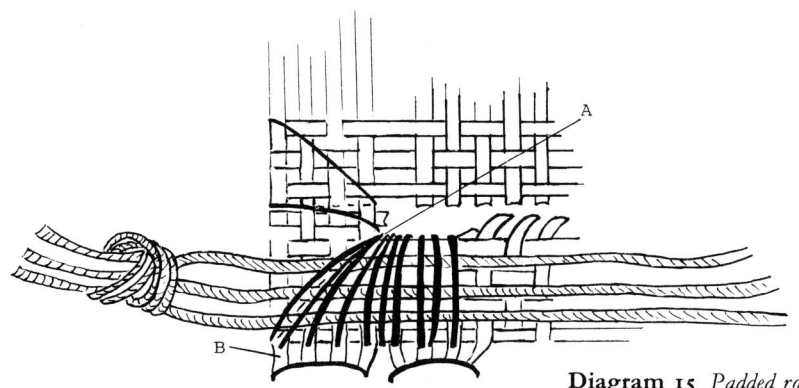

Diagram 15 *Padded roll*

loose, overlapped or given an extra tug to fix. The stitches must be upright and just close enough so that one cannot see the cord running beneath, but can still identify each stitch individually. During later stages, many connections are made into the roll so, if the roll is worked tight at this stage, it is possible that distortions will occur in the completed work. * Take the next stitch into the space at A, round underneath the four whipped threads and out into the first thread of the fabric to the right of the diagonal stitch at B. Repeat from * approximately three times. In order to maintain a closely whipped roll it may be necessary to go into the fabric threads more than once. Aim to spread the threads from the four-sided stitch out to the spacing they originally occupied before being worked.

It is now necessary to cut away the fabric from the inside area as the work progresses in advance of whipping. With embroidery scissors, cut no more than four threads at any one time along the line of the one drawn-out thread. Before cutting, push the fabric towards the centre; this will expose vertical threads that should then be cut as long as possible. These cut ends will then turn over in the direction of working and be incorporated into the roll to give added strength. Only one stitch must come out into the space between the four-sided stitch blocks; all others must make contact with the fabric as at B.

To finish and restart a whipping thread. At this stage move the padding cord to one side and make running stitches through the four threads still to be whipped. Begin a new length

of thread by running in reverse along the same threads and make a back stitch before coming out in the lower side where the next stitch has to register.

Continue to the centre three threads; *these must not be cut.* Work through these threads by working into the threads on the inside as well as the outside, keeping the roll continuous. Beyond these three threads begin to cut again, towards the next corner. Continue to whip until the needle comes out at the outside point of the diagonal stitch in the previous stage. In order to do this, stitches will pile up on the inside edge, but ignore this. Take the needle under and make contact with the fabric underneath, as at the beginning of this stage, before drawing the needle out and pulling this stitch up tight. Turn the cord at right angles and begin on the next side. Only one stitch actually forms the corner. When all sides are complete and the last group of cut ends worked in, cut off the knotted end of cord diagonally with the corner so as to form a mitre and continue until the last stitch lies close to the first. Cut off the cord ends diagonally, work one final stitch to settle over the top of the cut ends, pick up the fabric underneath as before and pull the thread up tight to draw the cut ends down out of sight.

To finish and restart a thread

To finish the thread in the previous example and any other thread from now on, take the needle through the roll at right angles to it, as in diagram 16, three times. Do not draw the

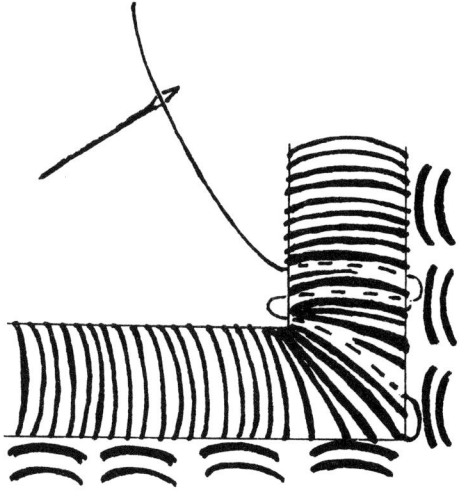

Diagram 16 *Finishing the thread at the end of the padded roll*

thread up tight but just close enough to prevent a loop of thread showing.

To begin a thread beyond this stage of the procedure, take the needle at right angles though a roll or bar in such a direction that the end of the thread, approximately $\frac{1}{4}$ in. (6 mm), will lie over or along the threads to be worked immediately. Take the needle back through, splitting the end of the thread in so doing, as shown in diagram 17. This anchors the thread sufficiently, so long as the end is worked in during the next operation.

To remove surplus fabric from the inside area

Cut along the line of one drawn-out thread that outlines the centre three threads, taking care not to cut the opposite three threads. Repeat once in the opposite direction. Now the four sections of fabric will easily pull free, leaving three threads in both directions. It will be noted that the original threads are now considerably looser than they were when the fabric was first mounted. This is because of the withdrawal of the opposite threads and this extra looseness must be maintained.

To whip square foundation bars

Whenever working over original threads one working thread is added. * Begin the thread as diagram 17. To lay an extra thread over the three originals, hold the leathercloth convexed so that the extra thread will be laid at the same tension as the originals, take the needle over to the other side of the square, out through the padded roll and back again. Hold the threads being worked at tension and horizontal to the worker. Now, work whip stitch, taking the needle under the foundation threads (now four) from above and working from left to right, as in diagram 18. Stitches will be at right angles to the four foundation threads, lying close without overlapping or being drawn up tight. Other threads will need to pass through this bar later so if worked tight it will cause

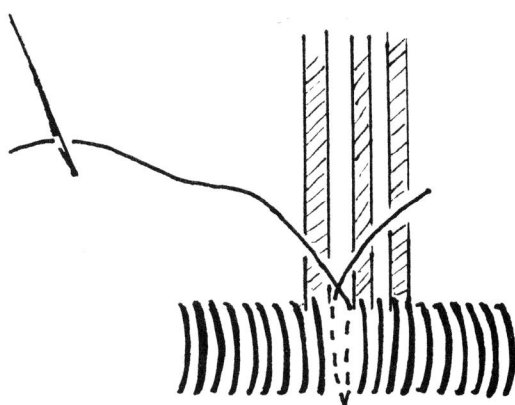

Diagram 17 *Beginning a thread*

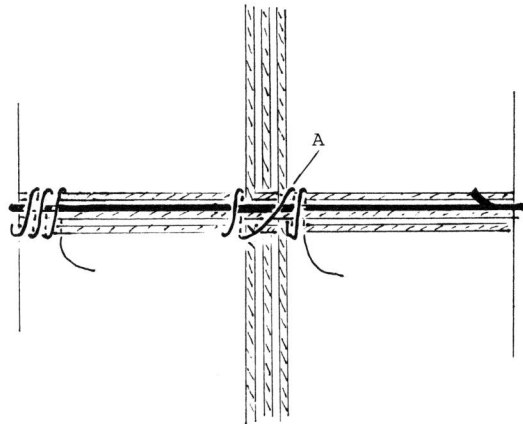

Diagram 18 *Whip-stitching square foundation bar*

difficulties and distortions. Continue towards the centre and up to the three opposite original threads. This junction must be fixed centrally. Maintain the natural spacing of the opposite original threads, take the thread diagonally over the centre junction, as at A in diagram 18, and continue to the end. Finish thread as in diagram 16 *. Repeat from * to * on the opposite original threads, taking the added thread under the half cross stitch at the centre junction. The cross will be completed as the second square bar is worked. Take care in centralising the centre junction.

To whip diagonal foundation bars

Begin the thread as before in a corner of the square and, as in diagram 19, lay the thread towards the opposite corner, taking the needle through the centre junction and holding the leathercloth slightly convexed so laying these foundation threads at the same tension as those of the square bars. Bring the needle through the padded roll at the opposite corner, take the needle back through the padded

roll and repeat until three threads are laid. Whip stitch as for square foundation bars, forming another cross stitch at the centre junction.

To work diamond foundation bars

These are not worked in all patterns but, when they are, they are worked at this stage of the procedure. Begin the thread as before, at the right-hand side of a square bar and into the padded roll, as at A in diagram 20. Lay the thread over to the next square bar in an anticlockwise direction. Take the needle through at the point where the thread passes over the diagonal bar, then to the left of the next square bar and out through the padded roll at B. Take the needle back through the padded roll, holding the leathercloth convexed so that the tension will be equal to the other foundation bars. Repeat to full circuit and then lay two more circuits and whip stitch, keeping diagonal foundation bars straight.

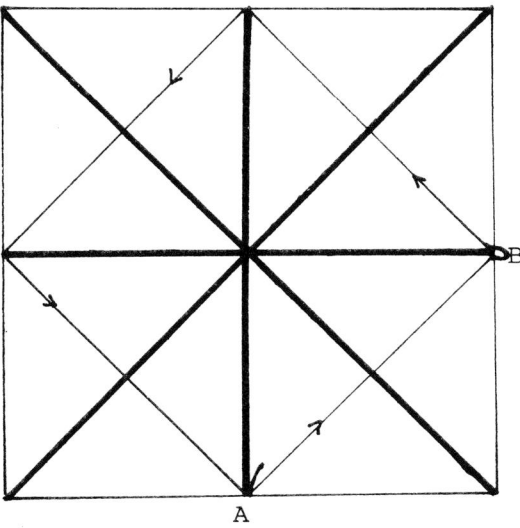

Diagram 20 *Laying threads for whip-stitched diamond bar*

To work woven square bars

This feature is usually worked over the three original threads when little or no part of the pattern occupies the square bars. This stage is

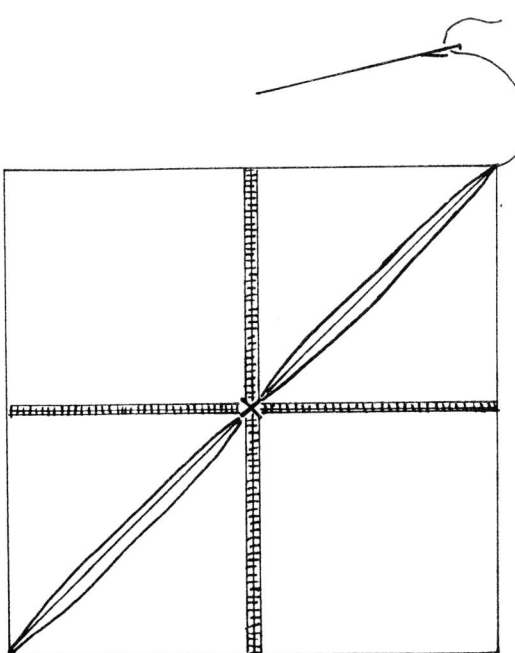

Diagram 19 *Laying threads for whip-stitched diagonal bar*

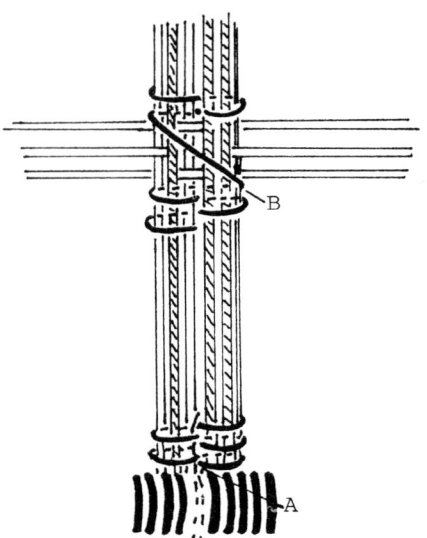

Diagram 21 *Woven foundation bar*

thread is now lying towards the right. Proceed as before to the end. Finish the thread as in diagram 16 (*see p. 26*). Lay the threads in the opposite direction, as before, but taking them under the half cross stitch at the centre junction: otherwise repeat as for the first bar.

To work double buttonhole-stitched bars

This feature can be applied to a variety of situations and is sometimes worked over an already whipped bar when this feature is not required over the full length or circuit of foundation threads. The type of buttonhole stitch used throughout this craft is also known as button stitch or blanket stitch, therefore it is the type without a twist, as is shown in diagram 22.

If this feature is worked over the three original threads, then one working thread is added. Begin thread as before, add an extra thread as before and hold threads to be worked in a horizontal position and at tension. Work the buttonhole stitch slightly spaced, as at A, to allow a buttonhole stitch to fit in between from the other side. Continue to the end, secure thread as at B and return along the other side as illustrated. Finish the thread as before.

worked after the completion of the padded roll. The weaving is worked over six foundation threads, so a further three threads need to be added.

Begin the thread as before in order to lay the extra threads parallel to the originals; two threads are laid on top of one original thread and one thread is laid on top of the other two original threads, taking care not to spread the width that the originals occupy, as in diagram 21. Bring the needle back through the padded roll and between the two columns of now three threads, as at A. Hold the threads to be worked over next in a vertical position. * Take the needle to the right, around behind and up through the middle of the two columns. Take the needle to the left, around behind and up through the middle again. Wrap the threads closely and pack stitches depthwise just close enough to cover the foundation threads*. Repeat from * to *, towards the centre and the opposite three threads, making sure they are central. Take the needle to the right, as before, and then to the left but, instead of coming up through the middle, take the needle straight across behind the six threads, as at B. Coming out at the right, take the needle diagonally over the centre junction to the left, behind the left-hand column and up through the middle. The

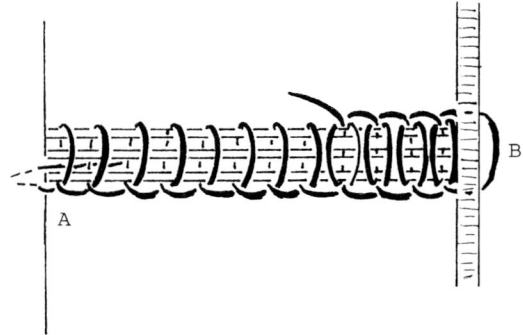

Diagram 22 *Double buttonhole-stitched foundation bar*

Drawing threads for an insertion

All the pattern areas in this craft are based on a square. There is no limit to the multiple so long as the shape follows the grain of the fabric. In the case of an insertion the total length of the pattern will be a multiple of the depth. This can be an odd or even number of repeats, depending on the type of pattern or patterns to be worked. If an alternate pattern repeat is to be worked, then an odd number of repeats will be required. If one or a running pattern are to be worked then either an odd or an even number of repeats can be worked – the area for plotting will probably determine which. There are three methods of plotting this shape, depending on their situation.

Insertion as an independent shape

This is usually widthways as at A in diagram 23, to fit between two outer borders, when the shape will be plotted from the centre to the ends. First find the centre of what is going to be the length of the insertion. The repeat is called a unit. The unit measurement will be

Figure 7 *Traycloth or place mat using linen spun and woven by hand by the author. It illustrates an insertion plotted as an independent shape, using the same pattern as a running repeat.*

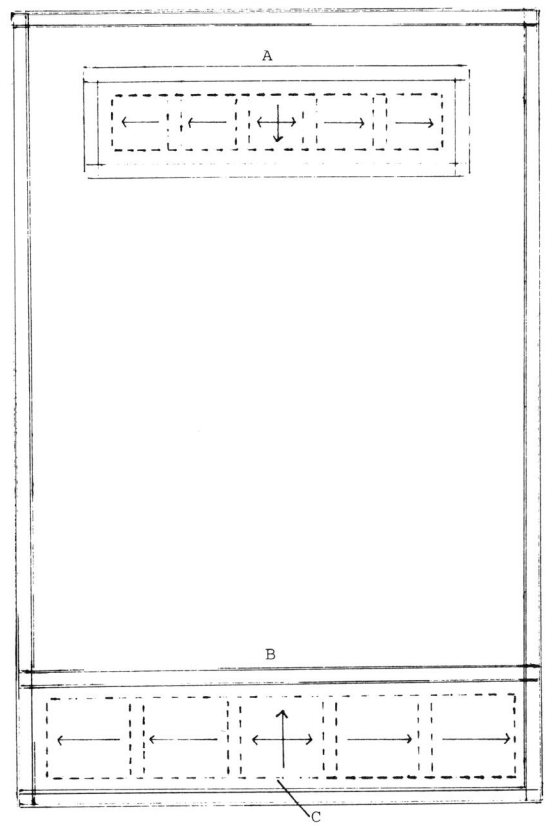

Diagram 23 *Drawing threads for an insertion*

determined by the number of repeats required within the given distance. It will often take several attempts at plotting before a unit size that will fit is determined, therefore do not get scissor-happy. If an odd number of units is required, as in diagram 23A, centralise the unit measurement over the centre mark on the fabric. Pick up on a pin the first and last thread of the unit, * leave three, pick up one, plotting towards one end of the insertion. The next

29

unit begins with the last one thread picked up. Pick up the last thread in the unit *, repeat from * to * as required. Leave four threads (for the padded roll) pick up two, leave four, pick up two (for the four-sided stitch border). If the first plotting is not satisfactory, then alter the unit measurement accordingly. The minimum margin between the end of a shape and any other border is eight threads. Now plot the other half, to make sure the initial centring was correct. Decide on the depth of margin from the end of the article. This need not be the same as that at the ends of the shape; the eye will help to decide a good balance for the size of the article being made. Pick up two, leave four, pick up two, leave four, pick up one, plot unit as before, pick up one (being the last thread in the unit), leave four, pick up two, leave four, pick up two. If an even number of units is required, then three threads form the initial centre. Pick up one thread on each side of the same, this thread being the beginning of the unit; otherwise continue as above.

Cut the one thread picked up from next to the border on all sides, and draw back to form a rectangle. This outlines the inside pattern area. Cut the one thread on either side of the three which separate the units and draw back to just inside the one forming the rectangle. Now cut and draw threads for the four-sided stitch border around this rectangle as for the square. This is now ready for the four-sided stitch to be worked, as described on pages 19–20 and in diagrams 5 and 6.

Insertion occupying the full width of the area between borders

This must be plotted before the four-sided stitch border is worked. Leave the four threads immediately next to the border at each end, pick up one (this will be included in the unit) and plot from the centre as above. Leave four threads, as in C, diagram 23 and plot the unit as before. Pick up one (this is the last thread included in the unit), leave four, pick up two, leave four, pick up two. The single threads picked up immediately next to the border are now cut and drawn back to form a rectangle. Cut the single threads on either side

of the three which separate the units, draw back to just inside the one forming the rectangle. Cut and draw the threads for the fourth side; these threads are drawn back to interlock with the border on the adjacent sides. Here an isolated block of four threads will occur and will be worked as one block when working the four-sided stitch border. It is possible that blocks immediately before will not be multiples of four threads – refer to the working of four-sided stitch.

This is now ready for the four-sided stitch to be worked, as described on page 19 and diagrams 5 and 6.

Insertion circumjacent to the outer border (Figure 8)

Here the fabric cannot be cut to size until two sides of the article have been plotted. Begin at one corner of the fabric, allowing for the required depth of hem (as in diagram 1 *see p. 17*) on both sides of the initial right angle. Plot the threads for the depth of border required, then leave four threads for the padded roll. Pick up one thread, as at A in diagram 24, plot the unit as before, picking up the last thread at C; *leave four threads* (this is because these same four threads will be used for the padded roll on the inside of the insertion — *see figure 8*) and pick up one. Continue to plot as in the previous insertion (diagram 23 [B], *see p. 29*. Plot an odd or even number of units as required, until just before the last unit, when four threads are left again. The same situation arises as occurred at the beginning; pick up one as at D in diagram 24, plot the last unit, leave four, then plot the depth of the border and hem allowance and pick up one thread. This is where the piece of fabric can then be cut away. Having plotted in both directions, forming a square or oblong as required, check measurements and number of units plotted, then cut out the piece of fabric.

Return to the initial right angle and cut the border threads as at A in diagram 1 (*see p. 17*). Cut the next single thread on both sides of the right angle as at A in diagram 24, draw back to form the corner and draw the other cut end back to meet the single thread immediately inside the border, plotting at the other end of

Diagram 24 *Insertion circumjacent to outer border*

the insertion at B in both directions. Cut and draw one end back to form the second and third corner and draw the other end of the thread back to meet the corresponding thread from B; this forms the fourth corner.

Return, again, to the initial right angle, cut the next single thread in both directions at C and draw across to fall just short of the one already taken out at B. From the second and third corners cut the first single thread away from those right angles, as at D.

The threads picked up on pins on sides E can now be cut in the middle of the margin between A and C. Divide areas F into the same number of units separated by three threads. It will be noted that the other threads outlining the four threads are still to be cut. Cut these approximately $\frac{1}{2}$ in. (1.3 cm) inwards from A and D, only unpick towards these points. They are not drawn back in the other direction as it will be noted that these threads are part of the border threads on the inside border.

Figure 8 *A traycloth illustrating the plotting of an insertion circumjacent to the border, using Pattern 8.*

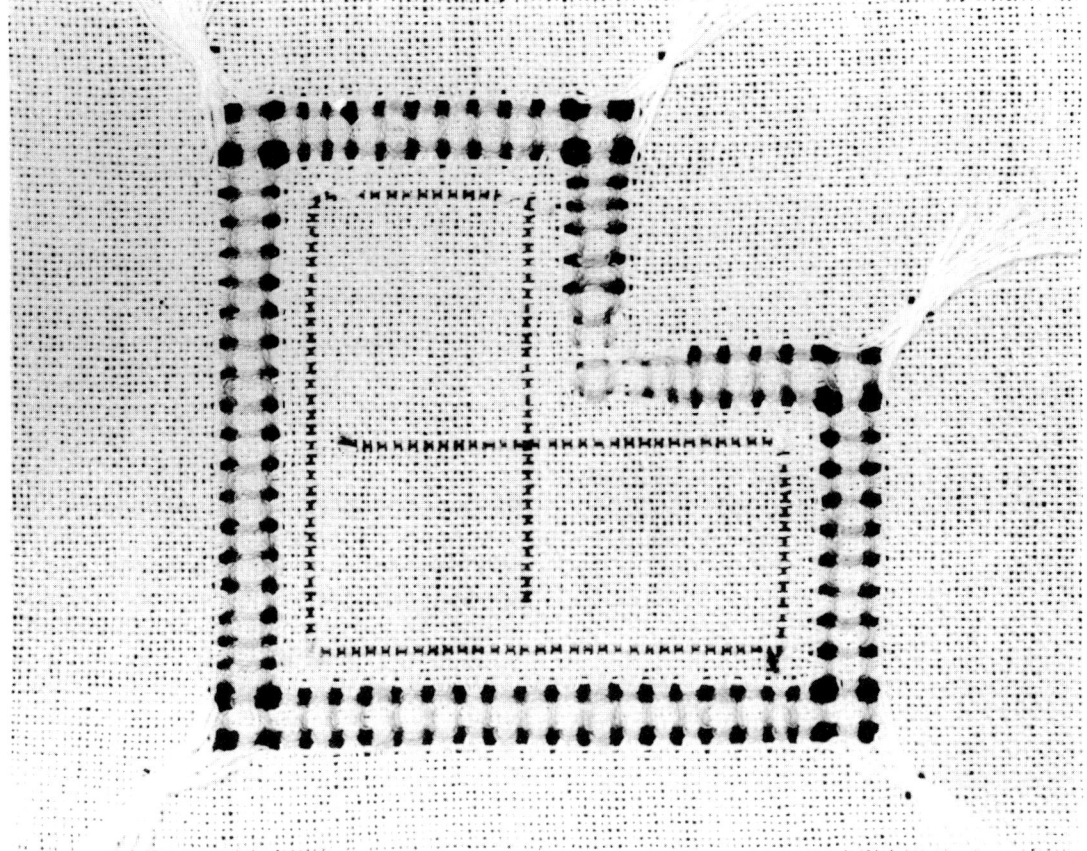

Figure 9 *Thread-drawing and the working of four-sided stitch at an inverted corner*

Now plot the border on the inside of the insertion: leave four threads for the padded roll, pick up two, leave four, pick up two. A single row of borders is advisable; deeper could be worked but it would detract from the pattern and cause an unnecessary weakness in the corners that really is not justified in the end result. When a padded roll is worked through an inverted corner, as at G, the point has to be built out. To make this easier, it is advantageous not to withdraw the border threads back to the corner but rather to leave them in and work the four-sided stitch, as in figure 9, and later the padded roll over the usual threads. This means that when the leathercloth is finally taken off these threads can be remove to expose a neat corner working, as in figure 8.

Work four-sided stitch on all borders. Mount on to the leathercloth, fixing the outer circuit first. Great care is needed here; check by measuring diagonally as well as on the straight to ensure a good shape and tension, as in diagram 13 (*see p. 24*), then fix the inner circuit.

The spaced whipping is worked in two circuits. Work the outer in the usual way, as in diagram 14 (*see p. 24*). The inner circuit is also worked as usual, except at the inverted corners, where the retained border threads are excluded; space whip over the usual threads, making a diagonal stitch over the corner with a block of four threads on each side of it.

There are two complete circuits of padded roll, the outer being worked first. The padding cords must be long enough to go round the

33

full circuit. Work the padded roll as in diagram 15 (*see p. 25*), taking care to retain the four threads where necessary and the three threads elsewhere. The inner circuit is begun in the corner, working from left to right and the stitches worked from the inside to the outside of the pattern area, just as for the outer circuit. Here corners are inverted and must be built up to achieve a right angle. Place the cord over the four whipped threads as before. Place the first whip stitch diagonally over the corner, picking up the fabric as before, but not pulling tight. Split each of the four threads to be retained on the inside of the insertion, bringing the needle out at the same place each time. Do not cut the threads on the inside until the last two threads retained in the opposite direction have been passed. Split the threads on the inside as well as on the outside; avoid making contact with the retained threads that run parallel; continue as usual towards the next inverted corner. Stop cutting on the inside when the first pair of retained threads in the opposite direction is reached; continue the padded roll, splitting the threads on the inside as well as on the outside. When the junction of the corner is reached, as at A in diagram 25, split each of the four threads which are to be retained for the foundation bar adjacent to C and D in diagram 24: work a diagonal stitch over the corner, picking up the fabric underneath (as at other corners) but, as this corner has to be built up, this stitch must not be pulled tight; split the next four threads, easing the cord around the corner to keep the bulk towards the point and bringing the needle out at A each time for the whole of the corner turning; begin to split the threads on the inside and outside again, until the last pair of threads retained in the opposite direction is worked. Begin to cut on the inside again; continue and finish as in the instruction for the padded roll, but without pulling the stitches tight, as in diagram 16 (*see p. 26*).

To remove the surplus fabric from the inside area, the fabric still attached on the inside of the inverted corner must be cut away close to the roll, avoiding, at all costs, the four threads that must remain.

The two bars of four threads in each corner

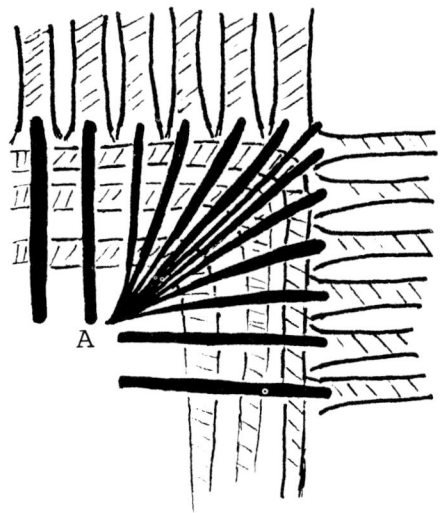

Diagram 25 *Padded roll at an inverted corner*

will both be worked in one operation. One working thread will be added if these threads are to be whipped or double buttonhole-stitched and two threads if they are to be woven. Begin the thread at one of the outer edges. Take the foundation thread in and out of the inverted corner to the other outer edge, return to the first outer edge and, using the same length of thread, whip or buttonhole stitch as required. This gives added strength to the point of the inverted corner.

Follow the order of working for the insertion or as the desired pattern indicates.

On completion of the pattern, it will be noted that there are no cut ends on the inverted corners so, therefore, the only corner neatenings are on the outer corners.

Remove the leathercloth. The threads that were retained at the inverted corners can now be withdrawn. First cut them close to the padded roll and then unpick the loose threads.

Order of working for insertions

Insertions are mounted on to the leathercloth as a whole. The padded roll is also worked as a whole. If the retained original threads that separate the units are to be whipped, a working thread is added, as in diagram 18, though, a feature can be made of these threads. If patterns are to be alternated or any other

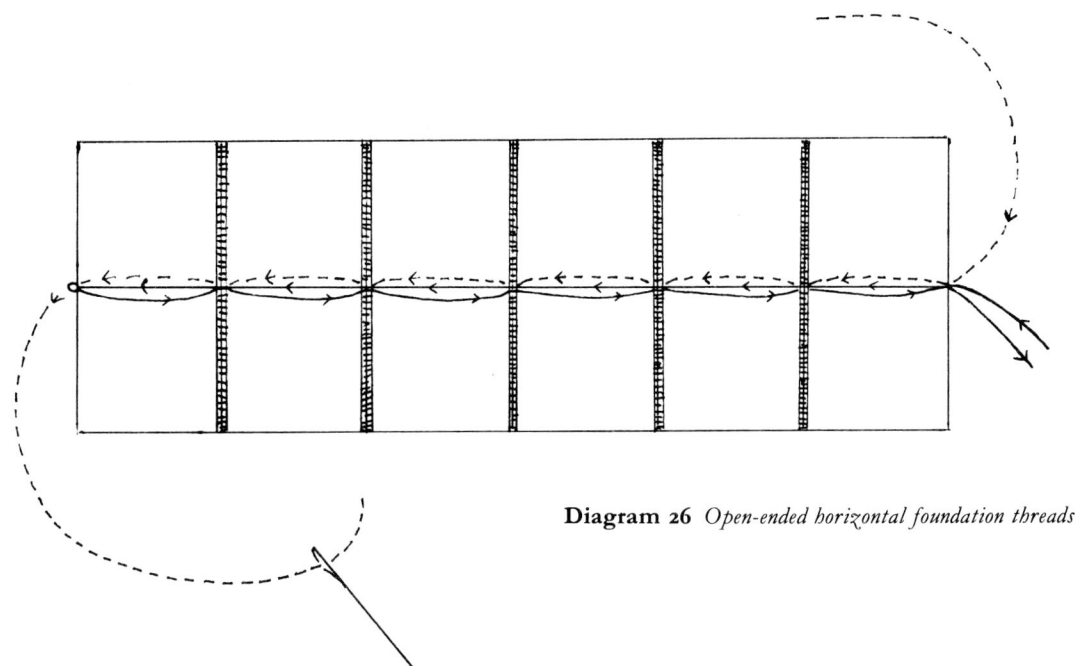

Diagram 26 *Open-ended horizontal foundation threads*

combination of patterns included, these original threads can be woven or double buttonhole stitched, as in diagram 21 or 22 (*see p. 28*). If the units are large enough to be divided into the usual eight sections, then proceed as described below. Each unit will be divided in half vertically (this represents one of the square bars), usually with a three-thread bar, and whip stitched.

To lay the horizontal threads
The aim is to do this in such a way that the threads across each individual unit can be tensioned as required (diagram 26). Measure the full length of the area plus a short length, which will eventually be used to finish off, and double this length – this provides two foundation threads. Using a Sharps needle begin to pass this thread from one end to the other from right to left and in a horizontal direction centrally through the verticals, leaving the end loose. Make the halfway point of the length of thread register at the other edge. Pass the thread through the verticals to the right and unthread the needle, leaving two loose ends. Take another piece of thread which is equal to the length, plus enough to work one complete

unit at the right, plus enough to use as a whipping thread. Take the third foundation thread through from the right, leaving a long end to whip one complete unit later and, with the remaining thread in the needle, begin to whip towards the right. This thread can be finished off and rejoined at any of the junctions. Tension the length through each unit, as with the bars, using the original threads as this foundation represents the other square bar. Finally, finish the whipping thread at the beginning of the last unit, using the longer of the foundation threads from the right to whip through the last junction. In this way, only two threads need to be finished off at any one position.

To lay and work diagonal foundation threads
These threads are estimated in the same way as for the horizontal bar, except that the measurement follows the diagonal through each unit and continues to the end of the insertion. So, again, the first thread provides double the required length plus enough thread to finish each end later. Other exceptions to the horizontal bar are that threads are only threaded through one unit at any one time and that the

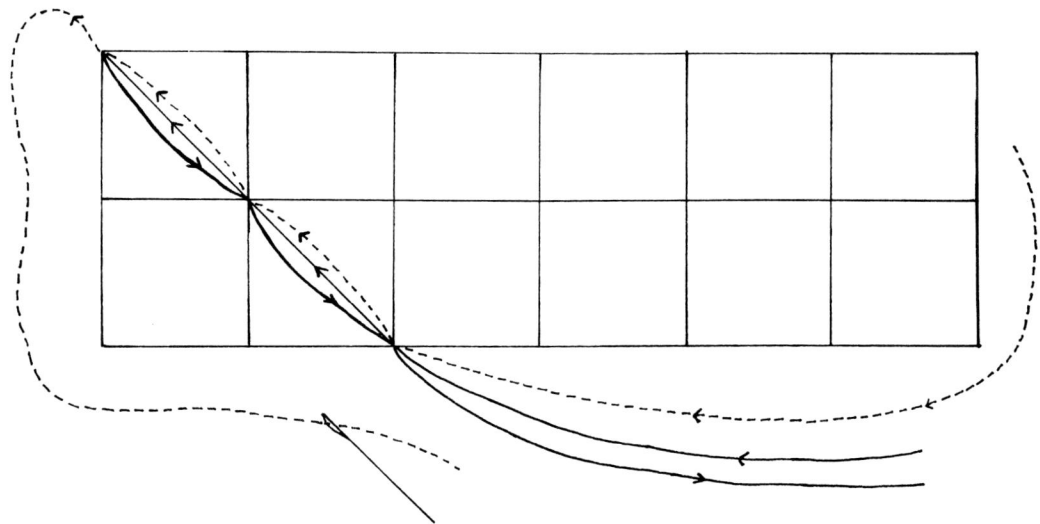

Diagram 27 *Open-ended diagonal foundation threads*

threads are whipped before passing them through to the next unit. In this way each unit can be tensioned as required.

Lay threads as in diagram *27* , whip across the one unit and take the needle through the padded roll to maintain the whipping tension. Keep this thread separate from the others if it is long enough to work another unit; otherwise finish it off now. * Thread needle with one of the foundation threads, take it back through the padded roll, coming out to the right of the vertical bar, pass through the centre junction and out diagonally at the other outside edge. Repeat with the other two foundation threads, whip and tension *. Repeat from * to * to last unit. Lay foundations as before, whip to the centre junction and finish off the whipping thread. With the long end of the foundation thread whip to the centre junction, tension and finish off the thread. Finish off the remaining two short ends into the padded roll.

Turn the work around so the other diagonal threads lie in the opposite direction and so that the finishing at the last centre junction will be at the other end of the insertion. If an unusually long insertion is to be worked, then this instruction is, of course, not practicable.

It is looking forward to this stage that urges the worker through the basic foundations; now she is ready to apply the pattern of her choice.

Remove the leathercloth.

Drawing threads for a right angle of units

This shape can be drawn in relation to a border or the right angle of a border, or it can interlock into the outer border or be drawn in complete isolation.

For the right angle to be plotted independently, the margin must be decided – again, this must consist of at least eight threads – and the unit size must also be determined, if only approximately.

** Begin to plot near to A in diagram 28. Locating threads for the four-sided stitch border and the single thread inside the padded roll threads as at A, plot the unit along the grain of

36

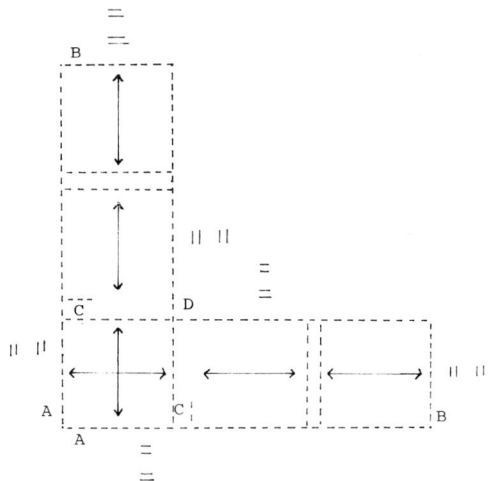

Diagram 28 *Right angle insertion*

thread to include the one thread picked up. Pick up the last thread in the unit, *leave four threads* (these will be the padded roll threads on the inside border of the right angle – see the photograph on the back cover), * pick up 1, plot the next unit, pick up the last thread, leave 3 *. Repeat from * to * until the last repeat: leave four instead of three for the padded roll, pick up two, leave four, pick up two **. Repeat from ** to ** in the other direction.

Return to the initial right angle. Cut the border threads as at A in diagram 1 (*see p. 17*). Cut a single thread on both sides of the right angle, as at A in diagram 28, draw the short ends back to form the corner and draw the other end back to the single thread at B which is now cut and drawn back to meet A. Return to the initial right angle again, cut the single thread at C, drawing the short end to meet A and the long end to reach B. This now completes the outlining of the inner pattern area. Cut the next thread along $\frac{1}{2}$ in. (1.3 cm) inside A and draw back to meet A. Cut the single thread on each side of the three threads separating the units. Continue to draw the threads around this shape for the four-sided stitch border, but not through the inverted corner at D (refer to the instruction for G in diagram 24 – see p. 31. Work the four-sided stitch border and proceed as for the instructions for

the previous shape, or as the desired pattern indicates.

Drawing threads for a multiple unit shape

This shape can be sited in the same situation as the previous example.

Plot the border threads and padded roll and pick up one thread at A in diagram 29. It will be observed that only the unit nearest to the intitial right angle is the correct size and shape and that there are four threads separating each unit.

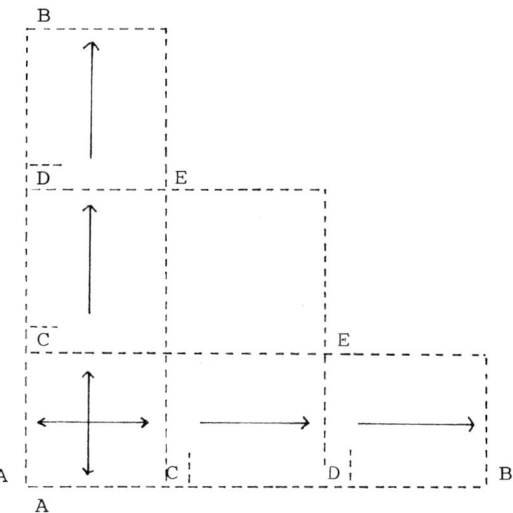

Diagram 29 *Multi-unit shape*

* Plot the unit, pick up one thread, leave four threads, pick up one *. Repeat from * to * twice more, picking up two on the last occasion. Leave four, pick up two, repeat from * to ** in the other direction.

Return to the initial right angle, cut both A threads and draw back to meet the B threads. Cut the B threads and draw back to meet A. Cut threads C and draw back to meet A and B. Cut the next thread $\frac{1}{2}$ in. (1.3 cm) inside A and draw back to meet A. Cut threads D and draw back to meet A and where both D threads meet. This now completes the outlining of the inner pattern area. Draw threads for the four-sided stitch border around this shape, except through the inverted corners at E (refer to the instructions for G in diagram 24 – *see p. 31*).

Work the four-sided stitch border and proceed as for the instructions for the insertion circumjacent to the outer border (*see p. 30*), as far as the working of the four-thread bars, when the threads from C and D in diagram 29 are worked together. Any other foundations will be determined by the pattern being worked.

Laying threads to form a circle

The direction of working in the main is from left to right, which, on a circle, is anticlockwise. When working whip or buttonhole stitch, the direction of the needle is from inside to outside, so as to be working with the arc.

The beginning of the threads in this situation differs slightly from the instruction given previously. Begin the thread as in diagram 30, at the required distance from the centre. Take

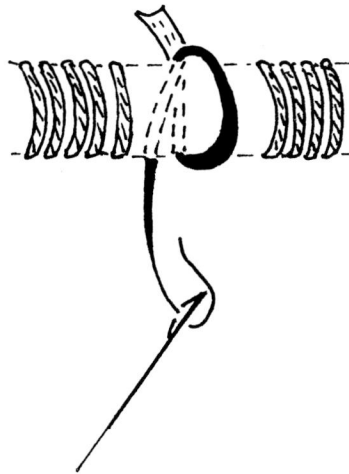

Diagram 30 *Beginning a thread for a circle*

the needle through a bar on the left of the centre junction in the direction of working, leave an end of thread approximately $\frac{1}{2}$ in. (1.3 cm) and take the needle through the bar again in the same place, splitting the end of the thread in so doing. Take the needle through each bar to register a good, full circle – a tight circle will register an octagon – and continue to lay two more circuits on top of each other,

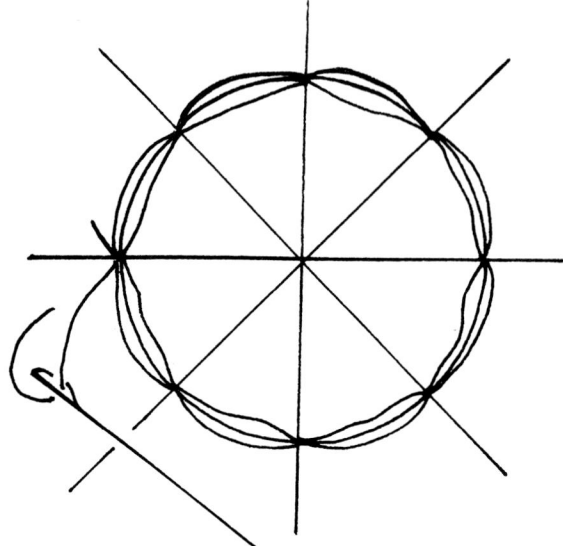

Diagram 31 *Laying threads for a circle*

as in diagram 31. With the same thread, length permitting, continue in the stitch required. Usually circles are worked in either whip stitch or buttonhole stitch; whichever is chosen, a stitch is worked on top of each bar in passing. A whip stitch forms a slanted stitch over the bar as at A in Diagram 18 (*see p. 26*). A buttonhole stitch is worked into and parallel with the bar being passed over.

If a one-thread bar is to connect into the circle, then an even number of whip stitches will be needed in each section to form a central space to accommodate the linkage later, as in diagram 32.

One-thread bars

This usually links a whipped bar to a buttonhole-stitched bar, as the latter is being worked, either as a circle or a straight bar.

The whipped bar usually has a number of whip stitches to accommodate a specific number of one-thread bars – for instance, for one one-thread bar, an even number of whip stitches will have been worked, e.g. four or six. These stitches will be slightly spaced so that the one-thread bar can settle in as another stitch. If more than one bar is to be linked to a whipped section then the number of stitches

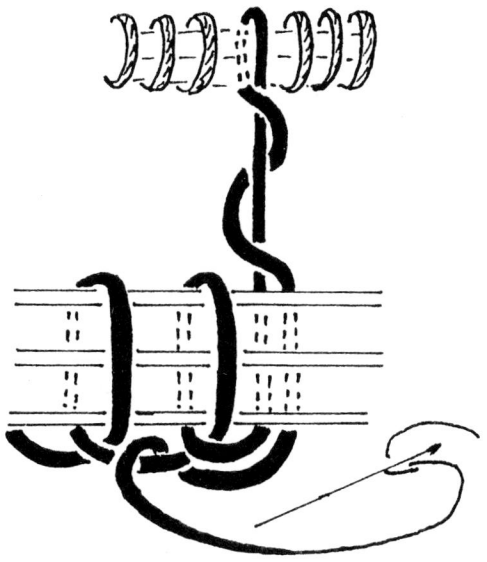

Diagram 32 *A one-thread bar*

Diagram 33 *First stage for a picot*

must be divisable by the number of bars to be added, plus one.

Lay threads for the second circle or bar no more than $\frac{1}{8}$ in. (3 mm) away from the first circle or bar and work in buttonhole stitch to where the one-thread bar is needed.

Take the needle under the buttonhole-stitched bar and bring it out in the space between the two bars, as in diagram 32. From above, bring the needle through the bar, between the whip stitches and towards the worker and draw the thread up to fix the distance between the circles or bars. Take the needle to the right and under the one thread. To the right of the one-thread bar bring the needle back under the buttonhole-stitch bar. From underneath, bring the needle up between the last two buttonhole-stitches. The thread is now back to where it set out. When only connecting a single one-thread bar, at this point work one less stitch than already worked, totalling an odd number of stitches.

Picots

These are only worked in conjunction with buttonhole stitch, often in the same position as a one-thread bar. The one-thread bar is com-

pleted first, followed by the picot between the same two buttonhole stitches. Picots add texture to a pattern or soften what may otherwise be a severe line or shape.

Take the needle down into the space between the last two buttonhole stitches, as in diagram 33, to form a chain stitch (with the thread travelling from right to left). Take the needle down into the chain, as if to make another chain and, before drawing it out, fold the work so that the needle stands upright and wrap the thread coming from the chain stitch round the needle closely three times in an anticlockwise direction. Hold the wraps with the first finger and thumb of the left hand. Withdraw the needle and draw the thread through completely. This makes the picot. To continue, bring the needle from underneath up between the last two buttonhole stitches back to where it set out, as in diagram 34.

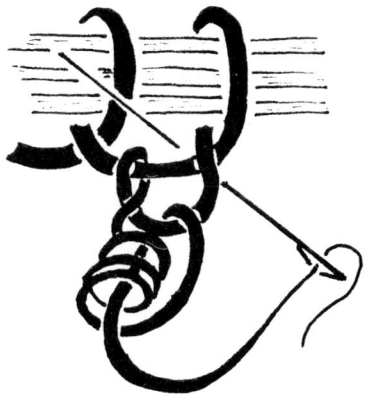

Diagram 34 *Second stage for a picot*

Petals

Petals are worked in various positions – on to three foundation threads, over an already worked bar, into a circular shape or on to a straight bar – sometimes having a one-thread bar linking them to another bar, which can be either circular or straight. The first row of a petal can be double buttonhole-stitched eventually, therefore the first row of stitches will need to be slightly spaced in order to take another row of buttonhole stitch from the other side after the petal has been completed: a picot could be worked here as well.

Begin by laying the foundation threads or by beginning the working thread, as necessary, to work from left to right.

First row: * work the required number of buttonhole stitches, working a one-thread bar from the centre stitch if the pattern requires it, in which case there will be an odd number of stitches.

Second row: take the needle to the left and down into the loop to the left of the first stitch at A in diagram 35 (this stitch is not counted), and out over the loose thread which is to be a

foundation thread for the next row; this thread must be left loose. Make a detached buttonhole stitch into the loop between each stitch on the previous row. There will automatically be one stitch less than on the previous row, as there is always one less in-between space than there are stitches.

Third and final row: take the needle to the left and attach as before into the loop to the left of the first stitch as at A in diagram 36. Make the first buttonhole stitch between two and three stitches on the previous row; leave the last space unworked to correspond with the beginning of the row. There will be three stitches less than on the previous row; this is the method of decreasing. Bring the needle up from underneath into the last empty space on the previous row at B. Bring the needle up from underneath into the space between the last two stitches on the first row. If the circle of these shapes is to be worked, work a buttonhole stitch on top of and parallel with the bar, to pass to the next section *. Repeat from * to *, length of thread permitting, otherwise finish the thread off as at A in diagram 37, in the bar slightly to the outside of the circle.

Re-join the thread, as at B, slightly to the inside of the circle. Take the thread through the bar so that the new end lies alongside the next section to be worked in, bring the needle back through the bar, splitting the end of thread in so doing, and pick up the buttonhole stitch on top of the bar so that the new thread is in the same position as the old one was before finishing. This method of re-joining will be used frequently.

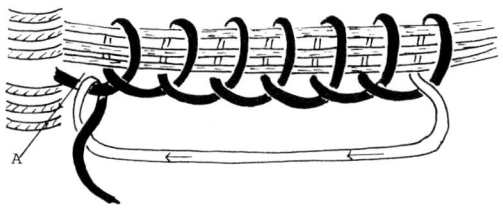

Diagram 35 *Attaching a foundation thread*

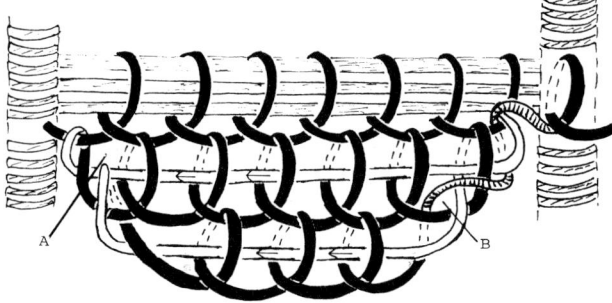

Diagram 36 *Petal*

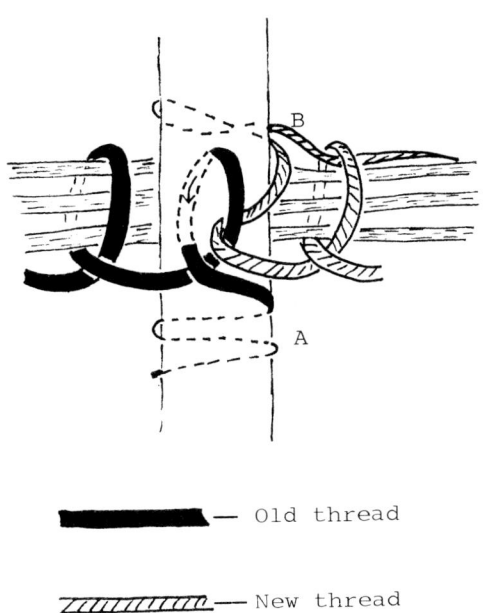

■■■■■■ — Old thread

⧄⧄⧄⧄⧄⧄ — New thread

Diagram 37 *Finishing and re-starting a thread to continue working*

Pyramids

These shapes are worked in detached buttonhole stitch and are preferably worked directly from three foundation threads; pyramids can be worked from a whipped bar, but are rather bulky. They can be tailored to fit into a specific area by decreasing stitches or by the tension of working, and can also be worked from a circle or a straight bar. Pyramids can also have picots worked on to the long sides: the one on the left is worked as the pyramid is worked, the other one as the right-hand side is whipped back up to the end of the first row. It will be noted that on some patterns picots appear on the inside of the circle from which pyramids have been worked. The stitches on the first row of the pyramid must be slightly spaced to accommodate a row of buttonhole stitches on the inside, when all the shapes are complete. Then work the picots.

Lay the threads, or begin a thread as the pattern requires, to work from left to right. Work the necessary number of buttonhole stitches over the foundation threads or bar. These should not be closely packed but just close enough so that the loop in-between the stitches can be located easily and so that the next row of stitches will not distort the shape.

Take the needle back to the left and down into the loop to the left of the first stitch, as illustrated in diagram 35. This foundation thread must be left loose, otherwise the shape will be narrow and it will be difficult to identify the space in-between. The tension of the buttonhole stitch will vary from worker to worker. This stitch can be drawn up as close as the worker feels necessary; so long as the foundation loop is sufficently loose, the next row will be worked satisfactorily. The worker may need to make several attempts before being satisfied with the end result. Resist the urge to discard the rejects; instead, attempt as many as necessary and eliminate only when all spaces are filled.

Bring the needle over the loose foundation thread as illustrated at A in diagram 35 and work a row of detached buttonhole stitch into the in-between spaces of the previous row, enclosing the foundation thread. For the next and successive rows, attach the foundation thread as at A in diagram 38. It will be noted that two threads are located here: one is the foundation thread of the previous row; the other, the thread which came to make the first stitch on the previous row. Locating both these threads ensures a good edge to the finished shape and firm anchorage for ease of working; there will automatically be one stitch less on each successive row. Continue in this manner to the last row of one, single stitch.

Pyramids need to be attached either to a padded roll or to a foundation bar. To attach a pyramid to a padded roll when the end of the pyramid is close to it, take the needle through the padded roll, and back through it from underneath, pick up the last single stitch worked on the pyramid and then, from underneath, work into the end stitch of each row. Finally, come up between the last two stitches on the first row. The thread is now back to where it began to build the pyramid. Work one buttonhole stitch on the next bar to the right. Finish the thread and restart as in diagram 37 if adjacent pyramids are to be worked. Always use a separate thread for each pyramid which has more than eight stitches on

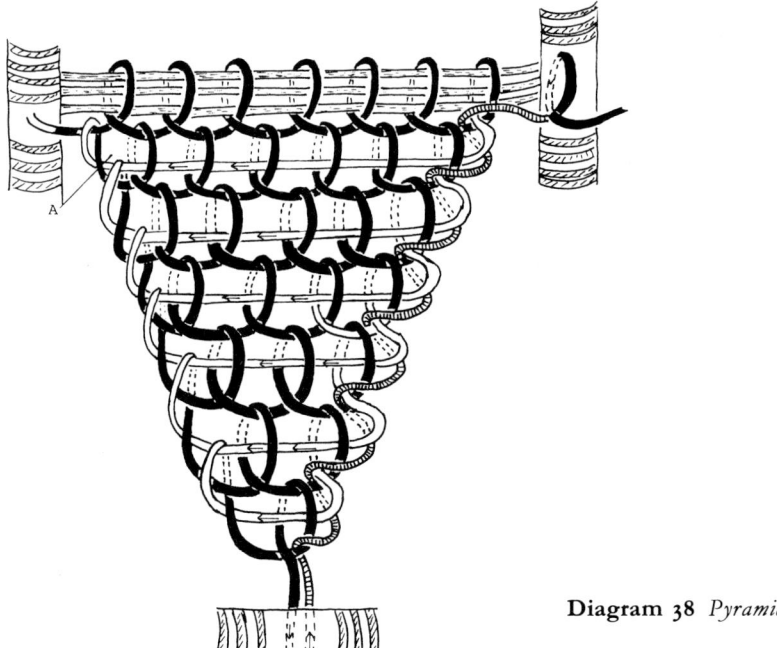

Diagram 38 *Pyramid*

the first row. If you are a beginner, always use a separate thread for each pyramid, so that any one can be eliminated independently if necessary.

Pyramids that do not reach the padded roll or foundation bar can be connected by a one-thread bar, as in diagram 32 (*see p. 39*). Finally, bring the needle up into the last, single stitch worked on the pyramid and complete as above. If the bar is to be longer than $\frac{1}{8}$ in. (3 mm), then three threads must be laid over the distance and whipped.

Sometimes it is necessary to work a pyramid with a foundation bar running underneath it. On the first row, work a number of stitches, as required, into the first section, single buttonhole stitch on top of and parallel with the bar involved and repeat the same number of stitches as in the first section; the total will be an odd number. The pyramid is worked completely free of the bar running beneath, so the number of stitches on the first row is treated as a whole. As the last, single stitch is being worked, pick up the bar at the same time; this secures the shape to the foundation bar. Then complete as above.

It may be necessary to decrease deliberately in order to tailor a shape to fit into a specific area. To do so, work as for the third row of the petal (*see diagram 36*). On successive rows, always take the foundation thread back into the loop to the left of the first stitch. There is a stepped edge on the left which will be rectified in the final whipping up the right-hand side, as above.

Bugs

These shapes are always worked over an already whipped bar – in groups or in isolation. Bugs can be as large as the situation allows. The end result always works out larger than the initial plotting of the first row of buttonhole stitches: this is because of the buttonhole stitches worked on top of the bar to make a continuous shape and to pass from one side to the other. The minimum number of stitches in the first row is five, otherwise the end result will be nondescript.

Begin the thread as in diagram 30 (*see p. 38*), at position A in diagram 39. *Work the necessary number of buttonhole stitches over

42

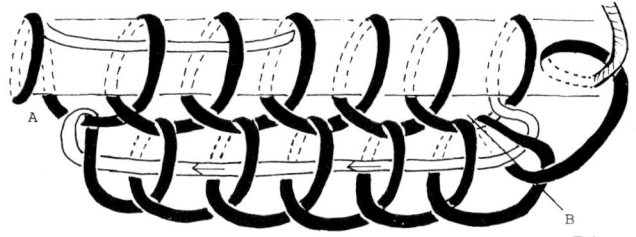

Diagram 39 *Bug*

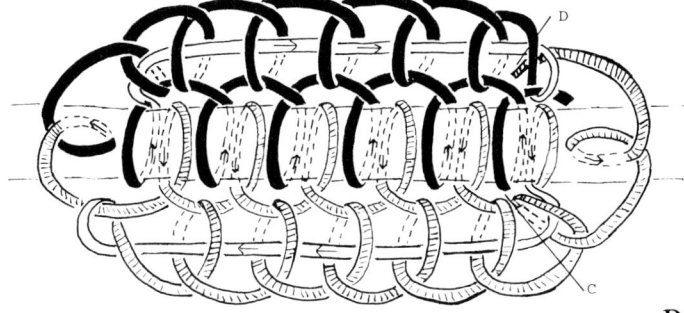

Diagram 40 *Second half of the bug*

the bar, taking in the end of the thread, and leaving sufficient space between the stitches to accommodate the first row of stitches on the second half of the shape. Take the needle back to the left and down into the loop to the left of the first stitch, as at A. Work a second row as in the diagram. Turn the work to the left so that the bar already worked is held vertically. Work another buttonhole stitch into the last in-between space; there are now two stitches in the same space, as at B. Then work one buttonhole stitch on top of the bar, parallel with it, and draw the thread out of this stitch vertically to close up the length in the stitch and give a firm outline to the end result *. Turn the work to the left again and repeat from * to *, taking up the spaces in between stitches over the bar already worked, in order to arrive at the same number of stitches as on the initial row. The last stitch will be between where the thread joins in and the very first stitch, as at C in diagram 40.

To complete the shape, bring the needle from underneath into the loop before the first stitch on the second row of the first half, as at D. To finish the thread, take the needle down to the underside through the shape and

through the bar already worked, taking care not to pull the thread so tight that it upsets the shape. Take the needle back and forth through the bar immediately under the shape to finish thread, or back and forth through the bar to work to an adjacent situation, if this is reasonably close, as in pattern 1 (*see p. 54*).

Weaving

This is needle-weaving over three uprights. This shape is always worked over a whipped bar, beginning at the end nearest to the centre of the pattern or point of radiation, as the beginning is usually thicker than the finishing end.

Begin thread as in diagram 30 (*see p. 38*), at A in diagram 41, working in the end of thread with the most convenient upright. Lay three foundation threads in an anticlockwise direction to form a shallow shape, as in diagram 41. Hold the work so that the foundations are in a vertical position with the working thread on the right at the base, as at A. Take the needle under the middle upright so that the first over stitch is on the foundation threads and can be tucked close up to the foundation bar so as to

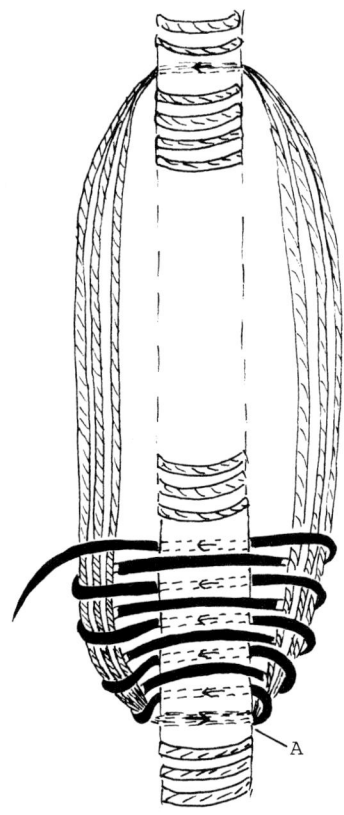

Diagram 41 *Weaving*

upright. Continue in this manner until no more stitches can be packed in. As the end approaches, the middle upright can no longer be picked up in one movement. The needle is then taken down under the middle upright and out towards the left and, in another movement, comes up between the middle upright and the left-hand upright. The rows should be close depthwise, so that no foundations are visible, with stitches wrapping the uprights without being loose but also without narrowing the shape. After the first few rows of weaving are worked, the three uprights should be parallel. If they are not, the three foundation circuits have been laid too loose.

Finish the thread as in diagram 16 (*see p. 26*), in the bar beyond the end of the weaving.

Oval buttonhole-stitched shapes

Begin the thread as for a circle, as diagram 30 (*see p. 38*). Lay the threads in an anticlockwise direction to form a shallow shape of three circuits. Begin to buttonhole stitch, continuing in an anticlockwise direction and making the first and last stitch in each half parallel with the bar already worked, as in diagram 42. Picots can be added to this shape. Take care not to draw the foundation threads through from the second half. Place one buttonhole stitch on top of the bar in order to pass from one half to the other. To complete: place one buttonhole stitch on top of the bar, bring the needle up from underneath between the first two stitches of the first half. Finish the thread as in diagram 16 (*see p. 26*).

cover the foundation threads. Take the needle over and under the left-hand upright and tuck this stitch close up to the bar. Pass over the middle upright and under the right-hand

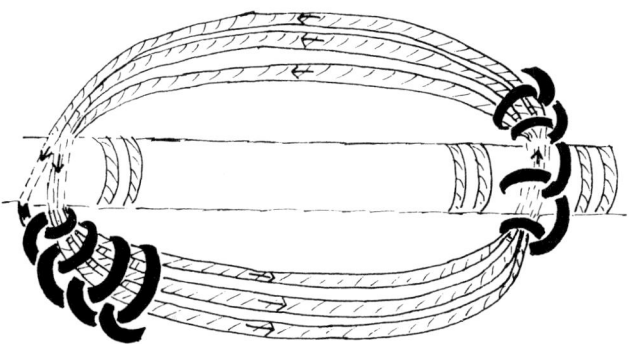

Diagram 42 *Oval buttonhole-stitched shape*

Bullion knots

Bullion knots are a typifying feature of Ruskin work. They are worked as a traditional edging; they also appear in clusters of eight in the centre of many patterns. Bullion knots can be added to give a textural effect or to eliminate a harsh junction of two crossed bars. In this case, a cluster of four can be worked or two laid obliquely over the junction. It is not good practice to work bullion knots in isolation over single whipped bars.

Bullion cluster of eight

Begin the thread by passing the needle back and forth through the underside of the centre to secure, then bring it up through the centre and draw the thread through. *Take the needle into one of the spaces between two foundation bars and up through the centre in the same place as the thread. Do not draw the needle out. Fold your work so that the needle can be held upright. Wrap the thread from the centre anticlockwise round the needle ten times as in diagram 43. Ensure the wraps are evenly twisted and come down to the base of the needle. With the thumb and first finger of the left hand, hold the ten wraps whilst withdrawing the needle and thread to its complete length. Now, hold the thread with the right hand and, with the help of the first finger nail of the left hand, curve the bullion knot to fit

into the selected space. Take the needle into the same section again and up through the centre. This completes the bullion knot and, with thread coming out of the centre it is ready for the next knot *. Repeat from * to * seven times more, but do not come up through the centre on the last repeat; instead, take the needle back and forth three times on the underside to secure the end.

Bullion knots worked obliquely

The direction of the oblique will be dictated by the pattern. Begin the thread as for the cluster. Bring the needle out at one end of the oblique, take it in at the other end and out at the same place as the thread. Wrap this thread ten times round the needle and complete as above. Make another bullion in the same manner as in diagram 44, following the same direction if the situation requires it. Finish as above.

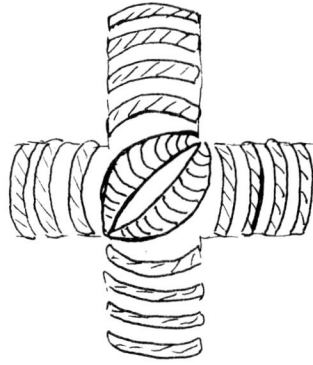

Diagram 44 *Bullion knots set obliquely on a junction*

Bullion knots as an edging

These are traditionally single, but they can be worked in pairs or trebles, when the third knot is laid over the top of a pair. Traditionally, single bullion knots are worked approximately $\frac{3}{8}$ in. (1 cm) apart, inclusive of the previous knot. Begin the thread at the far right-hand corner of the article, so as to be working from right to left as in diagram 45. Take the needle through the hem and bring it out two threads inside the outside edge of the fabric at the corner. Make a small stitch within the depth of these two threads and split the thread, bring-

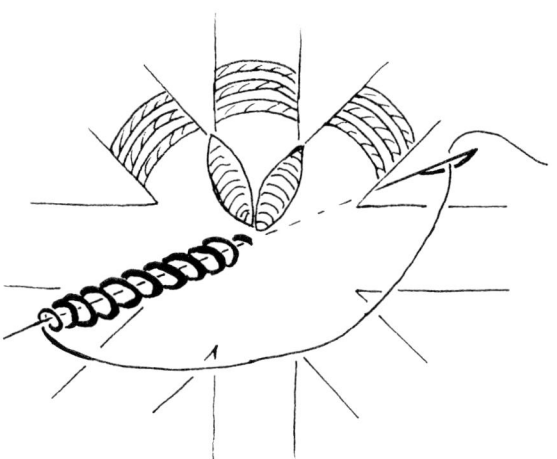

Diagram 43 *Bullion knot centre*

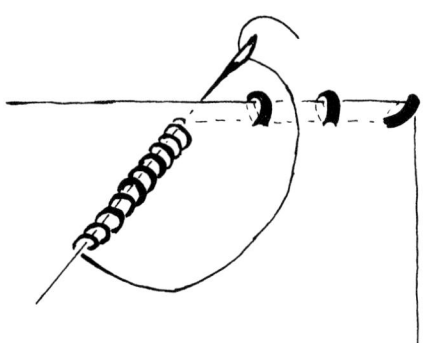

Diagram 45 *Bullion knot edging*

Diagram 46 *Woven centre*

ing the needle out at the same place again. Bring the needle up from the underside at the same depth. Before drawing the needle out wrap the thread round it twelve times in an anticlockwise direction. Hold, as for the cluster, draw the needle and thread through, curve the knot closely over the edge of the fabric and bring the needle and thread through to the right side, ensuring that the bullion knot is set diagonally over the corner. Take the needle and thread through the two layers of fabric of the hem to the next position, two threads inside the fabric edge. Bring the needle and thread out on the right side of the fabric and, from underneath, bring the needle up to take ten wraps. Complete and repeat as above. Continue towards the next corner of the article. Approximately 2 in. (5 cm) away from the corner, plot the distances so as to avoid ending with uneven spacing.

Woven centres

These are not frequently applied as they do not launder very well, but they are most useful where the article is going under glass when bullion knots would be too bulky.

Begin the thread as for the bullion knots in the previous section, and weave under and over the eight bars as in diagram 46. Because eight is an even number, the unders and overs will fall on the same bars each time. Work four circuits and finish the thread into the bar as in diagram 16 (*see p. 26*), at the outside of the completed shape.

This working is applied to a four-bar junc-tion, as in pattern 2; in this situation only three circuits are made – otherwise work as above.

To neaten cut ends

Scallop-shaped corner finishing is the traditional finish. This is worked where threads have been withdrawn for the working of the four-sided stitch border at the corners of squares, borders, or where borders are interlocked with the pattern areas. It is preferable to leave these corner workings until all handling of that particular area is completed, otherwise the finishing shape will become flattened and not so pleasing. If the long ends become a source of irritation whilst working the pattern area, they can be flicked through to the underside at any stage after the pattern area has been mounted on to the leathercloth, then returned to the right side for this stage.

Reduce the length of the cut ends to approximately $\frac{1}{16}$ in. (2 mm). Using a Sharps needle and working thread, begin at the left-hand end of the corner, as at A in diagram 47. Leave an end of thread approximately $\frac{1}{2}$ in. (1.3 cm) long and make a running stitch close to the inside edge of the corner, around to the right-hand end of the corner to B. Pick up the first thread involved in the first block of four-sided stitch, one thread deep into the fabric,

46

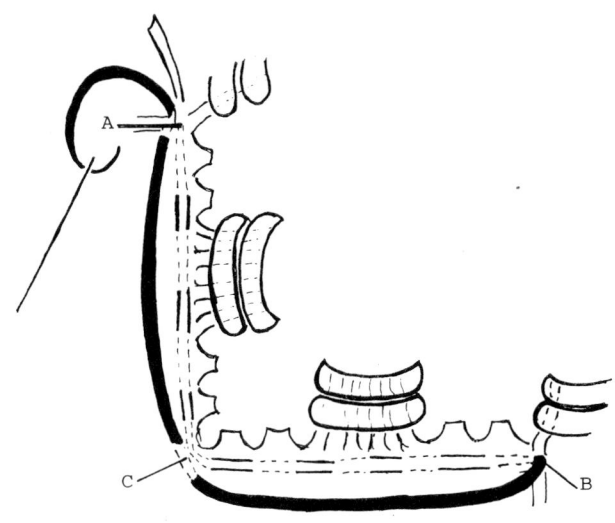

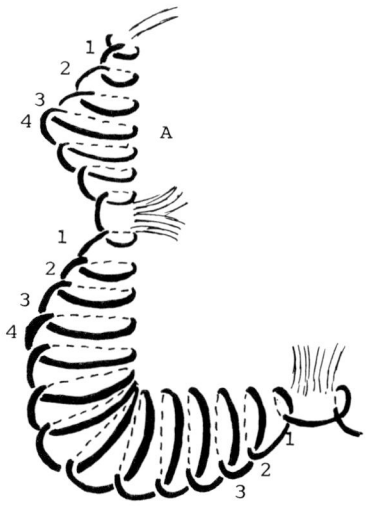

Diagram 47 *Corner neatening, stage one*

Diagram 48 *Scallop-shape corner finish*

and come back to the left in order to work buttonhole stitch, leaving the thread loose on top of the fabric and picking up a small amount of fabric at the corner as at C. Then, at the left again, pick up the first thread involved with the first block away from the corner, one thread deep into the fabric, as at A in diagram 47.

Beginning with a short buttonhole stitch into the space where the two threads have been withdrawn, increase the length of each stitch until four stitches are worked. Then reduce the length of the stitch, 3–2–1, making seven stitches into the same inner space as at A in diagram 48, to form a scallop or shell shape. Make the next buttonhole stitch into the outer corner space as before and increase the length of buttonhole stitch to the fourth stitch. Maintain the same length of stitch around the corner and make the stitches as close as possible. When back to the straight of the grain, reduce the length of stitch, 3–2–1. Make the next stitch into the next space and repeat the first shape.

To complete, take the needle to the underside of the work and finish the thread off by taking the needle back and forth through the backs of the stitches. When working this finish where a hem is involved there will be no backs of stitches, so finish the thread into the hem.

Where a double or multiple row of four-sided stitch border has been worked there will be a seven-stitch scallop for each pair of withdrawn threads either side of the corner.

Where borders have interlocked there will be a seven-stitch scallop for each pair of threads withdrawn.

Corners can be neatened with other finishes, one being a straight buttonhole-stitched shape. Prepare the corner as for the scalloped corner and work as far as returning back to the

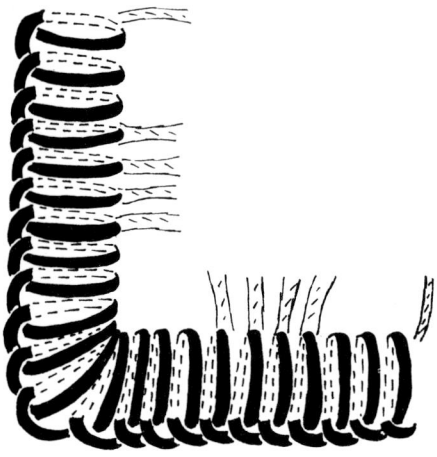

Diagram 49 *Straight-edge corner finish*

left with the loose foundation thread at A in diagram 47. Then, pick up the first thread two threads deep in the fabric, instead of one. Work a straight row of buttonhole stitch, two threads deep into the fabric, the whole way around the corner, as in diagram 49. Finish as for the scallop corner.

Removing the leathercloth

Once the worker is satisfied that the pattern is complete, it is time for the biggest thrill of all, especially on the first occasion, when it is finally proved that the pattern does not fall apart. The leathercloth is removed by cutting the back stitching on the underside of the leathercloth. This can be done quickly and without danger of cutting a wrong thread. The leathercloth will now peel away and any threads remaining in the four-sided stitch border can now be easily picked out. The same piece of leathercloth can be used many times, until it becomes too soft to maintain an area satisfactorily.

To press completed work

Ideally, this should be done before the bullion knot edging is applied. Roll the article in a damp towel, such as one that has been spun after washing. Place the whole thing in a plastic bag and leave to soak for a few hours, or preferably overnight, by which time the article will be evenly damp, and any surface soiling will have been dislodged. Unroll and place the article right side down on to a padded ironing surface. With a hot iron, *press*, do not iron; the use of steam is preferable but not essential. Press until the whole article is hot and steaming. To rectify any distortion, take hold of it at each side within the hem (otherwise the hem will become unnecessarily stretched) on the straight of the grain, and gently stretch. Repeat regularly down the length of the article and then do the same in the opposite direction. Return to the ironing surface and, with right-side down, continue to press, using the point of the iron to persuade any part of the lace work into the desired position. Whilst still damp, turn the article right-side up and gently smooth the fabric area, avoiding the pattern area. Stop before the fabric is completely dry. Lay the article flat where it can dry out. In this way, your article will be crisp and pristine without being shiny, especially if linen has been used. The author recommends pressing before resorting to washing. If work appears to have become unduly soiled during working, it is amazing how this disappears during the above process, and it should be repeated before deciding the article really does have to be washed.

The usual order of working

Always cut fabric out by drawn thread; this begins to rectify any distortion.

Work hems
The depth of hems will be up to the worker's personal preferences. Some articles will warrant a deeper hem on one or two sides – for example, with chairback covers and samplers a deeper, lower hem is effective while a deeper hem on the ends of long runners will give a well-balanced layout. Hems need tacking and slip stitching before drawing further threads. Draw further threads for the desired number of rows of four-sided stitch. A tip here: if the worker is anxious to work the patterned areas of the article, then just allow for the depth the required number of threads will take up. In

this way the spacing of drawn-out threads does not become distorted by others being misplaced. But it must be added that this only applies to the outer border where pattern areas are not involved. When laying out a patterned area on a large article, particularly a square article, it is advisable to lay tack lines at the centre; for a runner or a lampshade a central, horizontal tack line will be sufficient.

Lay out pattern areas

There are a few don'ts in this respect, the main one being: when planning a wall hanging or sampler, do not place a pattern right in the middle of the area and avoid the sides of pattern areas being lined up by the eye to make a continuous line. Patterns set on the diagonal plane will lead the eye into and around the pattern areas. Before being committed to cutting threads on an article that has a complex layout it is advisable to make a plan. Using a plain piece of paper the overall size of the article in mind, outline the hems and depth of border stitch. Use a different-coloured or patterned-paper which will be a contrast to the background for the shapes of pattern areas, to help arrive at a pleasing and well-balanced layout. Pattern areas can be any size, so long as they are square or a multiple of a square. Many patterns can be worked over varying sizes.

Work four-sided stitch

Work this around pattern areas, as diagrams 5 and 6 (see p. 20) or diagram 7 (see p. 21). If a woven corner is to be worked, as in diagrams 8 and 9, then it must be worked now.

Plot inside areas

This only applies to independent squares as in diagram 12.

Mount pattern areas on to leathercloth

When more than one row of four-sided stitch has been worked (see diagram 12), make the back stitch through the innermost row. For patterns plotted diagonally, use one piece of leathercloth and secure the largest right angle, so avoiding distortion of the diagonal plane.

Spaced whipping

As diagram 14 (see p. 24)

Padded roll

As diagram 15 (see p. 25). Remove surplus fabric from the inside area.

Square foundation bars

These are those bars using original threads, as in diagram 18 (see p. 26); for an insertion, refer to diagram 26 (see p. 35).

Diagonal foundation bars

As in diagram 19 (see p. 27), or, for an insertion, refer to diagram 27 (see p. 36).

Diamond foundation

As in diagram 20 (see p. 27). This is not worked in many patterns but, when it is, it is worked, at this stage. It will be noted that some patterns have further foundation bars. If the pattern also has a diamond foundation bar, the working of this helps in the alignment of those extra foundation bars. The working of the extra foundation bars would follow the working of the diamond foundation bar.

Patterns

When deciding which part of the pattern needs to be worked first, try to identify the part that is recognised at first glance. If that part is worked in proportion, regardless of the pattern drawing being the same size as the actual pattern area, the other components will either fit in or be adapted. For example, if there are pyramids or other dominant shapes, it is likely that these will need to be worked first. Work bullion knots last.

Neaten corners

As in diagrams 47 and 48 (see p. 47) or diagrams 47 and 49.

Remove leathercloth

Press

Part II

PATTERNS & EDGINGS

Patterns 1–60

John Ruskin brought the original patterns from Italy where he saw a similar type of work on church linen. We are not quite sure in what form these patterns reached Marion Twelves but, because of our methods of working, it is assumed they came in the form of line drawings. If not, it is felt that the method of working would have been to produce motifs, which would then have been applied to the fabric. It is most likely that pattern 3 was one of those originals, as it is very typical of the form of needlepoint John Ruskin would have seen in Italy.

Patterns have been handed down from worker to worker over the years. This collection is used mainly as an inspiration and a guide. As no two workers proportion in the same way or work at the same tension it is necessary to adapt and, in this way, new patterns are constantly being evolved, very often without the worker being conscious of the design, resulting in an original pattern; other students will work out their own patterns using graph paper and endeavour to reproduce them exactly in their work. Whichever method is adopted, it is hoped that the worker will enjoy the working and achieve satisfaction in reflection. When referring to diagrams always refer to the written instruction as well.

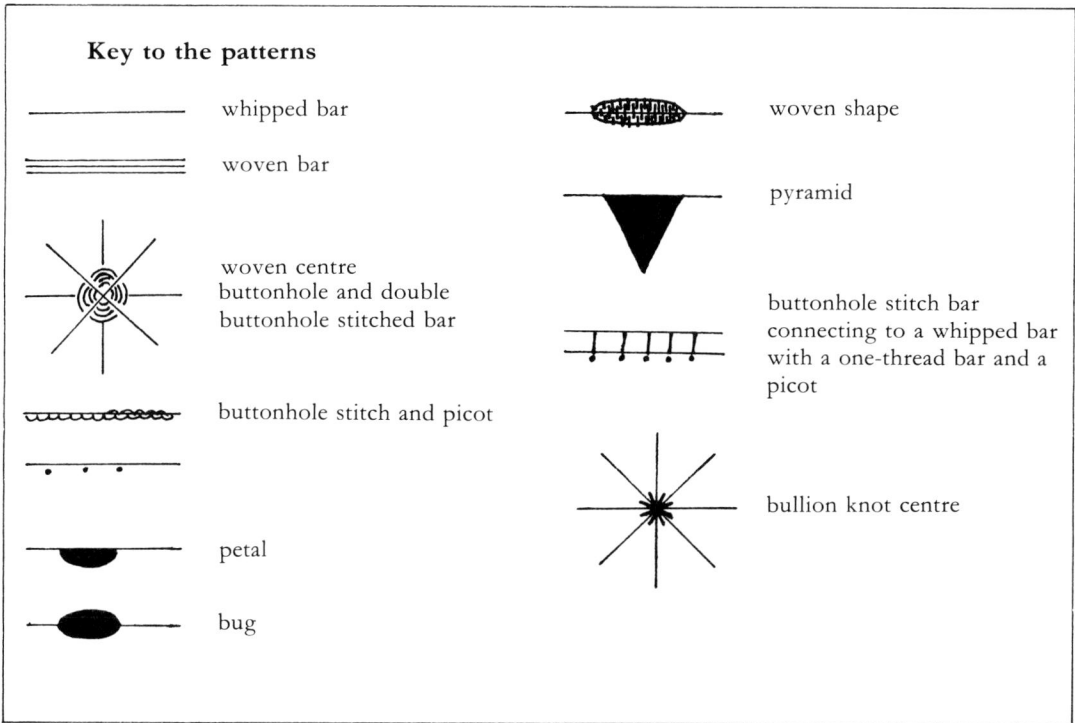

Key to the patterns

whipped bar

woven bar

woven centre
buttonhole and double
buttonhole stitched bar

buttonhole stitch and picot

petal

bug

woven shape

pyramid

buttonhole stitch bar
connecting to a whipped bar
with a one-thread bar and a
picot

bullion knot centre

Figure 10

Pattern 1

─────── 2¼ in. ───────

This is a good pattern for beginners as all shapes are small workings. Follow the order of working as far as and including the diamond foundation bar.

Plot the centre unit so that the petals will not touch the bugs. Begin with the centre whipped circle, approximately ¼ in. (6 mm) from the centre junction, as in diagrams 30 and 31 (*see p. 38*), working an even number of whip stitches in each section. Lay threads for the second circle less than ⅛ in. (3 mm) away. Work the petal as diagram 35, with a one-thread bar from the middle stitch on the first row. Complete petal as diagram 36 (*see p. 40*).

Work the bugs: begin the thread at the end close to the four-bar junction, as in diagrams 39 and 40 (*see p. 43*). Thread permitting,

54

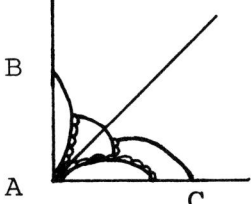

Diagram 50 *Corner working for Pattern 1, stage one*

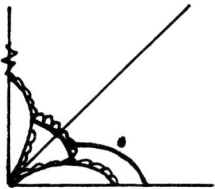

Diagram 51 *Corner working for Pattern 1, stage two*

instead of finishing after each shape, take the thread backwards and forwards through the bar and junction to the next position. The bug in this situation usually has six stitches on the first row. Take care not to let the bug on the diagonal bar encroach too near the corner and so restrict the corner working.

The small half circles are three threads and whip stitch beginning the thread at A in Pattern 1.

The corner working is rather complex: follow diagram 50. Begin thread at A, lay three foundation threads to form a shallow, curved shape approximately ⅜ in. (1 cm) long, work in buttonhole stitch and finish off thread. Re-join the thread at B, lay three threads to correspond with the first shape and work in buttonhole stitch to halfway. Then lay three threads to connect the two shapes, passing through the

diagonal bar, and pick up the thread between two buttonhole stitches to attach. Work two buttonhole stitches, lay three threads to point C, work in buttonhole stitch with a picot, as in diagrams 33 and 34 (*see p. 39*), at halfway point. Work to the connecting bar and work a third buttonhole stitch, then one on to the diagonal bar. Work three stitches on to the second half of the connecting bar and continue to B. Follow diagram 51, pass the thread backwards and forwards through the roll to the same distance between the corresponding two points, lay three threads and repeat as in the corresponding bar, finish the thread.

Work a bullion knot centre as in diagram 43 (*see p. 45*).

Neaten the corners as in diagrams 47 and 48, or diagrams 47 and 49 (*see pp. 47 and 48*).

Remove the leathercloth.

Pattern 2

———— 2¼ in.————

This is a pattern that was worked extensively in the early days of the cottage industry.

Follow the order of working as far as and including the diamond foundation bar.

Lay a circle of three threads for the innermost circle as in diagrams 30 and 31 (*see p. 38*), no more than a ¼ in. (6 mm) from the centre junction. Whip with an even number of stitches into each section. Lay threads for the next circle to work the pyramids, with a one-thread bar to link to the inner circle as in diagram 32 (*see p. 39*), on the first row of the pyramid. Ideally, all the threads for this unit should be laid so that the finished pyramids fall short of the diamond foundation bar. Work pyramids as in diagrams 35 and 38 (*see pp. 40 and 42*).

From the single stitch at the end of the pyramid take the needle through the diamond

Figure 11

foundation bar at a point that places the end of the pyramid equidistant between the square and diagonal bars. Take the needle out through the padded roll at the corner of the pattern and back again to lay three threads between the corner and the single stitch at the bottom of the pyramid. Whip stitch back up to the bottom of the pyramid and complete as in diagram 38 (see p. 42).

To work woven corners, begin the thread in the corner of the square and begin to weave as in diagram 41 (see p. 44), maintaining the spacing of the three uprights. Finish weaving towards the left, taking the needle and thread through the left upright, through the padded

roll and back to lay three threads through each upright to form an arc that will enclose the weaving. Work in buttonhole stitch with a picot in each section. It will be noted that the two outer sections require more stitches than the two inner sections.

Work the double half circles as for the full circle as in pattern 3.

Work a woven centre as in diagram 46 (see p. 46), with smaller weavings at the junction of the pyramid bar and the diamond bar, but only work three circuits.

Neaten the corners as in diagrams 47 and 48, or diagrams 47 and 49 (see p. 47).

Remove the leathercloth.

Figure 12

Pattern 3

——— 2¼ in.———

This is probably one of the patterns that John Ruskin brought back as a drawing.

Follow the order of working as far as the diagonal foundation bars.

Lay a circle of three threads halfway from the centre to the outside edge on the square bars, as in diagrams 30 and 31 (*see p. 38*), taking the thread through the other seven bars at the same distance from the centre.

Work the pyramids over these foundation threads with (here) 11 stitches on the first row, as in diagrams 35 and 38 (*see pp. 40 and 42*).

Lay a circle of three threads for the innermost circle, as in diagrams 30 and 31 (*see p. 38*), and whip with an even number of stitches in each section. Lay three threads for the second circle and work in buttonhole stitch. From the centre stitch in each section work a one-thread bar and then picot as in diagrams 32, 33 and 34 (*see p. 39*), working one buttonhole stitch on top of the bar in passing to the next section. Repeat a quarter of this unit in each of the corners.

Work a whipped, inverted V-shaped bar over three foundation threads at the outer ends of the square bars.

Work a bullion knot centre as in diagram 43 (*see p. 45*).

Neaten the corners as in diagrams 47 and 48 or diagrams 47 and 49 (*see p. 47*).

Remove the leathercloth.

Pattern 4

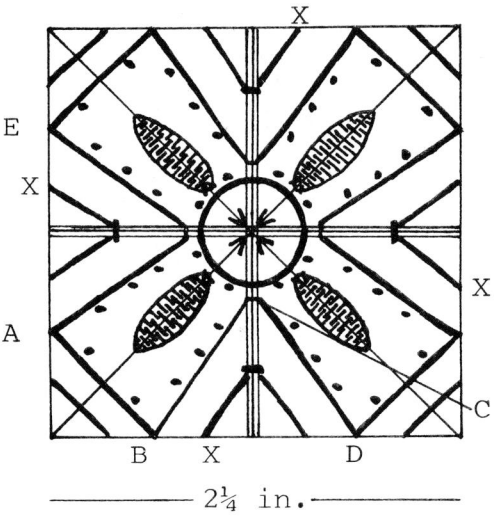

———— 2¼ in. ————

This pattern has woven square foundation bars. These can be a feature of any pattern where worked shapes are not applied to the square bars, except perhaps where a circle of eight pyramids is to be worked; this would then break the formation into four quarters.

Follow the order of working as far as the padded roll, then work woven square bars and diagonal foundation bars.

Begin the thread at A, which is halfway from the corner to the square bar and trace the thread to B; where the thread has passed over the diagonal bar, take the needle and thread through, then out through the padded roll at B. Bring the needle back through the padded roll at B so that both threads are emerging at the same point on the inside edge of the roll. Take the needle and thread through the woven square bar at C and out through the roll at D.

Repeat from A to the full circuit and lay two more circuits. Work in buttonhole stitch and picots, as in the pattern, to the inside in a clockwise direction. Place two buttonhole stitches on the woven bar, one into each column of weaving. At E, carry straight on to the next bar; linking the last buttonhole stitch and the first one on the next bar holds the buttonholing in position. Continue to the full circuit. Threads can be finished and re-started at any position into the padded roll as in diagram 37 (*see p. 41*).

Lay the inner circle of three threads; work buttonhole stitch and picot.

Work woven shapes as in diagram 41 (*see p. 44*).

Work a bullion knot centre. Because of the width of the woven bars, the bullion knot cluster will form four pairs.

Whipped straight bars are worked at the corners.

Inverted V bars at the outer ends of the square bars are whipped with a bullion knot lying over the width of the woven foundation bar. Lay three threads beginning at X, whip up to the woven bar. Take the needle and thread through the woven bar, take the needle through again but, before withdrawing, make bullion knot of ten twists, and withdraw the needle. The knot will now lie over the width of the woven bar. Bring the needle and thread through again to secure the knot and continue to whip the second half of the shape.

Neaten the corners as in diagrams 47 and 48 or diagrams 47 and 49.

Remove the leathercloth.

58

Figure 13

The next 12 patterns are useful for working on to place mats or to fill awkward areas on a sampler or lampshades. They can also be worked as alternatives in the centre four units on a window pattern. Some of these patterns can be worked into squares varying from 1 in. to $1\frac{3}{4}$ in. (3.5 cm to 4.5 cm).

Pattern 5

After the basic grid, the diamond bar threads are laid as in diagram 20 (*see p. 27*) and worked in buttonhole stitch and picots or double buttonhole stitch if this pattern is to be worked in a larger area or on a lampshade. Work the square next; this will be whipped. The inner circle can now be fitted into the remaining space. To work the corner units, lay three threads to form a quarter arc, buttonhole stitch, with one stitch on the bar (*see C in diagram 50, p. 55*). To complete second half arc, see diagram 51, p. 55.

Pattern 6

The centre unit of this pattern is worked as the centre unit of pattern 3, but without the picots. For the outer shape, begin the thread on the outside of the shortest square bar (if there is one) and pick up just the loop of the buttonhole stitch from which the one-thread bar was worked on the inner unit, then through the diagonal in an anticlockwise direction at the same distance from the inner unit as on the previous bar. Lay three circuits and work in buttonhole stitch – picots can be worked, if the worker so desires. At the junction of two loops, make the last buttonhole stitch close to the inner unit, turn the work and make the next stitch into the next loop.

Pattern 7

Begin the thread on a diagonal bar. Lay a square of three circuits and work the first row for the pyramids slightly spaced in order to accommodate a row of buttonhole stitch immediately inside later. The first row consists of a number of stitches in the first section, one stitch on top of the bar and the same number of stitches in the second section as in the first. The pyramid is worked free of the bar running underneath except on the last row, when the bar is picked up as the last stitch is being worked. Complete as usual. To work the corner unit, lay three threads so as to be able to work buttonhole stitch from left to right as in diagrams 52 and 53. It will be noted that the foundation threads for the third loop do not pass through the bar. Attach the third loop to the bar with a buttonhole stitch and continue straight on from the third loop to complete the second loop.

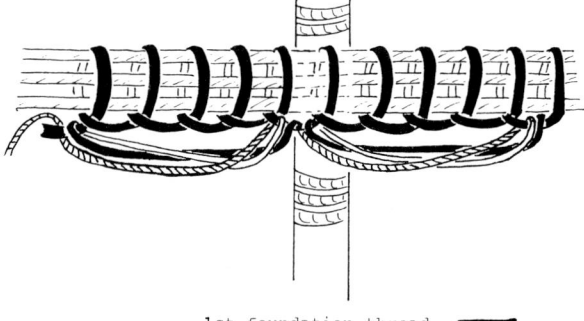

1st foundation thread ▬▬▬

2nd foundation thread ═══

3rd foundation thread ▨▨▨▨

Diagram 52 *Lay three-thread loop*

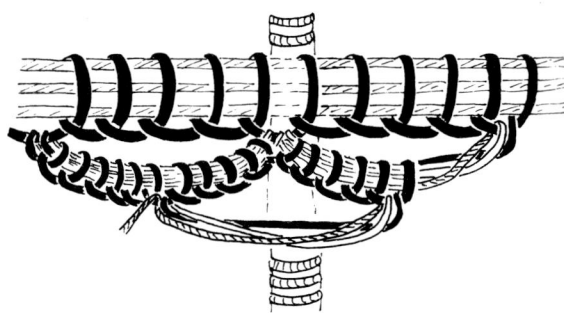

Diagram 53 *Three-loop shape*

Pattern 8

The pyramids are worked first. Lay three threads across the corner. Where the pyramid ends determines the size of the inner circle.

Pattern 9

To work the pyramids: begin the thread for the foundation threads on a diagonal bar, so as to be at the beginning of a row on the completion of the three circuits for one of the pyramids. The picot is worked on to the left

edge as the pyramid is being worked. Attach the foundation thread in the usual way. Into the same place, make a detached buttonhole stitch, then make the picot, then bring the needle up from underneath into the same place yet again and proceed to work the row and complete the pyramid. In this case, the pyramid is being worked with the square bar running underneath, to which the last stitch of the pyramid is attached. Whip up the right side and, in doing so, make the second picot to correspond with the other, making a detached buttonhole stitch into the end stitch of the same row. Complete as in diagrams 38 and 37 (see p. 41). It is advisable to use a new thread for each pyramid.

Pattern 10

This pattern is as for the centre unit of pattern 1 (see p. 54).

Pattern 11

The inner circle is worked first and is usually whipped. Work the bugs as in diagram 39 (see p. 43), beginning thread at the circle end.

Pattern 12

Proportion the pyramid circle as for pattern 3 (*see p. 57*).

Pattern 13

In this pattern the thread is begun on the square bars and stitches will be slightly spaced to accommodate an inner circuit, when pyramids are all complete, with a picot in each section. It may be necessary to decrease the number of stitches on this inner row, missing an in-between space when working the buttonhole stitch into which the picot will be worked.

Pattern 14

Lay three threads as in diagram 20 (*see p. 27*), work a pyramid directly on to them towards the centre of the pattern. It will be necessary to decrease on nearly every row in order to tailor the shape to fit within the square bars. To do this refer to the instruction for the working of a pyramid (*see p. 41*). In this situation, it is often necessary to work two bullion knots set obliquely over the centre.

Pattern 15

The centre circle is whipped but, on enlargement, buttonhole stitch and picot could be worked. Work the petal as in diagrams 35 and 36 (*see p. 40*), spacing the stitches on the first row to work buttonhole stitch and picot on the other side later. Begin working the petal near to the circle.

Pattern 16

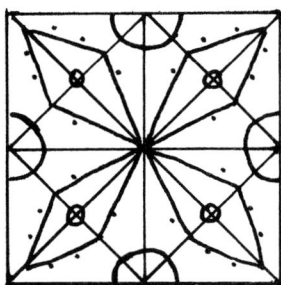

Work the basic grid, including the diamond foundation bar. Begin the thread at one of the outer corners, pass through the diamond bar, then through the centre in an anticlockwise direction to form a figure of eight for the foundations only. Work in buttonhole stitch with picots, passing the thread through the centre on the first shape and placing stitches on top for the second shape.

Patterns 17 to 22 can be worked into areas varying from $1\frac{3}{4}$ in. to $2\frac{1}{4}$ in. (4.5 cm to 5.6 cm).

Pattern 17

The shapes in this pattern are explained in Patterns 1 and 9 (*see p. 54 and p. 61*).

Pattern 18

Lay three threads for the outer square, work three rows as for a pyramid and then the three loops as in diagrams 52 and 53 (*see p. 60*).

Pattern 19

The threads for the inner square need to be laid so that the pyramids finish well short of the end of the square bar. This allows the border to be laid and worked leaving a margin between it and the pyramid. This corner working is useful when there is a large area to fill. Work as for the corner unit of Pattern 3 (*see p. 57*). After working the first one-thread bar, lay threads and work as for the corner unit of Pattern 1 and diagram 51 (*see p. 54*). Continue to the next one-thread bar. Lay the threads through the diagonal bar and into the loop between the last stitch of the previous shape and the first one on the arc and work this loop, complete the arc and take the thread back and forth through the padded roll to complete the whole shape.

Pattern 20

The pyramids must be completed by halfway along the diagonal bar. Work the pyramids from the corners first: in this way the trials and errors will be independent, with the opportunity of four attempts, by which time the worker will know the size of the circle to lay. After the second pyramid has been attached to any bar and before whipping up the right side of the pyramid, make a bullion knot over the bar. The scallop loop shape is worked, basically, as in diagrams 52 and 53 (*see p. 60*). Always buttonhole stitch to the last half loop on each row, finally attaching the whole shape to the square bar as the end loop is worked. Complete by working the last half loop of each row back to the base line.

Pattern 21

Work the pyramid to attach it to the padded roll with a one-thread bar if the distance is less than ⅛ in. (3 mm). Otherwise, lay three threads and whip. Lay threads for the loops to the inside of the pyramids, as in diagram 52 (*see p. 60*) but in a clockwise direction. The size of the inner circle will be determined by the remaining inner space.

Figure 14

Pattern 22

The inner unit is as Pattern 1; the scalloped buttonhole-stitched shape is laid as in diagram 52 (*see p. 60*). Begin the thread into the petal and work in an anticlockwise direction passing the threads through the bar. Lay the threads for the complete circuit before buttonhole-stitching. The corner unit is as Pattern 5 (*see p. 59*).

Patterns 23 to 28 can be worked into areas varying from 2 in. to $2\frac{1}{2}$ in. (5 cm to 6.3 cm).

Pattern 23

Work the pyramids, laying the circle so that they finish to allow the shallow-arced circle to follow. The pyramids are left suspended until all eight are complete. Begin the thread and lay the threads as for Pattern 6 (*see p. 60*), passing the thread through the end stitch of each pyramid. To work the connecting bar between the pyramids, bring the thread up through the edge of the pyramid on the right, split the end of the thread and pass it through the bar to the left. Pick up the edge of the pyramid on the left to correspond, lay two more threads and work in buttonhole stitch. Finish the thread by whipping down the edge of the pyramid.

Pattern 24

Lay the threads to work the inner circle so that the next circle can be at halfway on the square bars. Whip with a number of stitches divisable by three or four and lay threads for the pyramid circle, working two or three one-thread bars on the first row. In the illustration the pyramids reach the outside edge; if this does not happen in practice, it is preferable to make a one-thread bar rather than distort the circle. For the double buttonhole-stitched snowflake centre, begin the thread at the outer end, in such a way that the thread emerges from the circle, and buttonhole stitch towards the centre, making a picot where there is most space — usually two stitches from the outer end. Make the last stitch close to the centre, * turn, work anticlockwise to the next bar and buttonhole stitch and picot to the outside. Take the needle through the circle then through the bar and back through the circle to work double buttonhole stitch — in this way the buttonhole stitch will be prevented from twisting later — return to the centre, making the last stitch beyond or to the centre of the first stitch *. Repeat from * to * completion. The linkage between pyramids is a matter of personal choice, using the method described in the previous pattern.

Figure 15 *Traycloth illustrating an independent insertion linked with a border, using Patterns 23 and 26 alternated*

Pattern 25

The main unit is made up of two four-pointed star shapes. Begin the thread on the outside end of the square bars and, in an anticlockwise direction, take the thread through the diagonal to fix a deep pointed shape. Complete three circuits and work in buttonhole stitch. Begin the thread on the outer end of the diagonal bar at the same distance from the centre as for the other shape. Take the threads through the other shape where they cross and place a buttonhole stitch on the top. The inner area will determine the size of the circle.

Pattern 26

Work the main unit as for pattern 6 (*see p. 60*). Work the inner circle; this could be nearer to the centre than illustrated. Work the oval buttonhole-stitched shape as in diagram 42 (*see p. 44*), and the corner as Pattern 5 (*see p. 59*).

Pattern 27

Work the outer circle of three-looped shapes, allowing for double buttonhole stitch later, then work the next innermost circle of shapes. The double buttonholing on both these circles can now be completed. The remaining area will determine the size of the inner unit.

Pattern 28

Buttonhole-stitching on the diamond bar makes for easier attachments later. Whip the inner square. Work the pyramids so that they attach the diamond bar. The distance between the attachment of the pyramid to the diamond bar and the diagonal bar determines the length of the loop which, in turn, determines the size of the other shape.

Patterns 29 to 34 can generally be worked into areas from 2–3 in., (5–7.5 cm) some can be worked into even larger areas.

Pattern 29

This pattern has extra foundation bars which divide up the circular grid radiating from the inner circle. Lay the inner circle and work with buttonhole stitch outermost, and with an even number of stitches slightly spaced into each section. Lay the threads for the extra bars. Beginning the thread in the padded roll at a point that divides the circumference, attach the thread to the inner circle by picking up the central loop of the buttonhole-stitching. Having laid three threads, whip stitch. Lay threads

for the outer circle beginning on a square bar. Note the distance from the centre. Register at the same distance from the centre on the other bars to complete three circuits. Buttonhole stitch to the inside on one section only using an even number of stitches. Refer to diagrams 52 and 53 (*see p. 60*), and work to halfway on the third loop. This is now a template to determine the position of the last circle. Allowing for a short length of one-thread bar, lay the threads for the last circle and whip stitch. Return to the template, attach it to the finished circle and complete as in the instructions for diagrams 53 (*see p. 60*) and 37 (*see p. 41*). Repeat 15 more times. Work woven shapes on to the basic foundation bars the full distance between the first and third circles, beginning the thread at the centremost end. Work double buttonhole stitch on alternate bars with a picot two stitches from the outer end. Work an inner circuit of buttonhole stitch and picot on the first circle and an outer circuit on the second circle. To work the corner shapes, begin the thread at the halfway point and lay the threads for a shallow buttonhole-stitch shape, as in diagram 42 (*see p. 44*), innermost. Complete, then lay threads for the second shape which will be smaller

Pattern 30

This pattern is not easy and should not be attempted until the worker is really familiar with her tension. The completed pyramids need to end parallel with or slightly inside the centre one-thread bars on the two adjacent shapes.

Pattern 31

Work the centre unit attaching pyramids to the padded roll with a three-thread bar. Whip stitch and complete the pyramid. Lay threads for the petal circle; the linking buttonhole-stitch bars can be worked at the same time as the petals.

Figure 16

Pattern 32

Lay threads for the pyramid circle and work the pyramids, attaching them to the padded roll with a three-thread bar – if it is to be longer than $\frac{1}{8}$ in. (3 mm) – or else a one-thread bar. Work the inner unit for Pattern 6 (*see p. 60*), minus the inner whipped circle.

Pattern 33

After the diamond foundation bar, lay and whip three threads to form the right angle to secure the pyramid foundation threads. Lay continuous threads for the undulating bar, at a distance for the pyramids that is slightly less than halfway on the right-angle bars. Work the pyramids and outermost buttonhole stitch, followed by a complete circuit inside. Work the centre unit as for pattern 10 (*see p. 61*).

Pattern 34

Again, this is a pattern best left alone by beginners. Lay threads for the outer circle and work the pyramids. Lay the next innermost circle and work a pyramid towards the centre of the pattern, placing the necessary number of one-thread bars; where the pyramid ends determines the centre circle. Work this, then attach the pyramid and proceed with the remainder.

The next 12 patterns are called window patterns; they have an extra foundation grid which divides the square grid into 16. Work to the diamond bar of the basic foundation grid; in some patterns threads only are laid at this stage. Lay the threads for the extra bars in line with the junction where the diamond bar threads pass through the diagonal. These patterns are useful for moderately large areas where the lace work is to be mounted on the bevel, as on a pincushion. The extra grid ensures regular attachment to the padded roll, thereby preventing it from being pulled out of shape. These patterns can be worked into square pattern areas from $2\frac{1}{2}$ in. to 3 in. or $3\frac{1}{2}$ in. (6.4 cm to 7.5 cm or 8.8 cm).

Pattern 35

After working the extra foundation grid, lay the circle for the pyramids as in Pattern 13 (*see p. 62*). Where the pyramids end determines the size of the circle; it is preferable not to have less than six stitches on the first row of the petals. The small circles need to be very small; as there are only four spokes it is difficult to maintain a circle unless it is small and the stitches are closely packed.

Pattern 36

The centre unit is as Pattern 35 but the circle is slightly larger. The double buttonhole-stitch shape is as Pattern 24 (*see p. 66*), but begin the thread at the centre so as to work in an anticlockwise direction. Work the bullion knot on the end as in Pattern 4 for the inverted V bar (*see p. 58*).

Pattern 37

Work the groups of pyramids as Pattern 9 (*see p. 61*), with or without the picots. The centre unit is two whipped circles laid close together, then bullion knots worked close together passing through both circles.

Pattern 38

After the window foundation grid, it will be noted that there is yet another foundation bar to complete the grid: a V that completes a diagonal cross in the two squares on each side of the pattern. Work the centre unit as in Pattern 10. When working the corner petal unit lay the threads for the right-angle bar at the same time or continuously.

Pattern 39

The foundation threads for the pyramids are laid as a rectangle along the diagonal plain. Work the pyramids as in Pattern 14 (*see p. 62*). Remaining foundation threads are whipped and form the other diagonal in the outer corner squares.

Pattern 40

The centre unit is as Pattern 9 (*see p. 61*), with a circle large enough to allow the pyramid to reach beyond the window grid junction. Lay the threads for the corner unit and whip stitch other than where picots are required. Then work as the corner unit for Pattern 2 (*see p. 55*).

Pattern 41

This is very straightforward: the units are as in pattern 13 (*see p. 62*).

Pattern 42

This pattern again is very straightforward: the centre unit is as Pattern 13 (*see p. 62*), and the petal units are three-quarters of Pattern 10 (*see p. 60*).

Pattern 43

This is one pattern where the diamond foundation threads are left unworked until after the window bars are completed. The pyramids are now worked in the direction shown in the illustration. The centre unit is as Pattern 13 (*see p. 62*), and the bugs as in Pattern 1 (*see p. 54*).

Pattern 44

The three foundation threads for the pyramids are laid in a continuous circuit. The pyramids are worked as in Pattern 14 (*see p. 62*), and the centre unit as in Pattern 13.

Pattern 45

The diamond foundation threads are dealt with as in Pattern 43 (*see p. 77*), but with the pyramids worked in the other direction. The threads for the independent pyramids are laid at the same time as working. The centre unit is as in Pattern 10 (*see p. 61*). Note the woven shapes need to begin at the outer end and fall short of the petal unit.

Pattern 46

The square immediately inside the four centre squares is worked in buttonhole stitch and one-thread bars; the corner arcs, except the last one, can be worked at the same time.

The following two patterns are suggestions to be used for insertions or right angles, as illustrated, repeating or adding units as desired into unit sizes from $\frac{7}{8}$ in. to $1\frac{1}{2}$ in. (2.2 cm to 3.8 cm). For the foundation grid procedure refer to the order of working for insertions, as in diagrams 26 and 27 (*see p. 35 and 36*).

Pattern 47

Lay the foundation threads for the pyramids using the same method applied in diagram 27 (*see p. 36*), where pyramids are not required, the threads are whipped. The double buttonhole stitch and picots are worked after the pyramids, continuously from one shape to another as much as possible.

Pattern 48

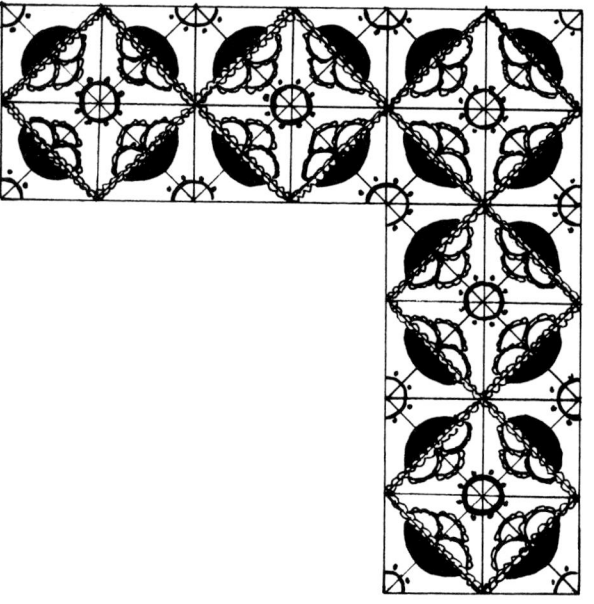

Lay the foundation threads for the double buttonhole-stitch diamond grid, following the same method as applied in diagram 22 (*see p.*

The next two patterns are suitable for small multi-unit areas, for unit sizes ranging from $\frac{3}{4}$ in. to 1 in. (2 cm to 2.8 cm).

Pattern 49

28). Work single buttonhole stitch along the entire length before beginning the double buttonhole. To work the petal shape, count a number of in-between spaces to the *right* of the diagonal bar. Begin the thread in the next outermost space by bringing the needle from underneath and splitting the end of the thread. Lay the foundation thread to the left, leaving the same number of spaces in between to the left of the bar. Work two rows as for a pyramid. On the third row, decrease as in diagram 36 (*see p. 40*). Complete as for the petal and take the needle through the double buttonhole-stitching. Lay the foundation threads for the two base line loops in the same manner as in diagram 52 (*see p. 60*), but, because it is necessary to begin at the left, when the three threads are laid the needle is at the wrong end so a fourth thread needs to be laid. Complete as in diagram 53 (*see p. 60*). The remaining inner area determines the size of the circle, which, in turn, determines whether or not a bullion knot centre is necessary.

To lay the foundation grid, which is all whip-stitched, refer to diagram 54. A and B are the original threads to which one thread is added as in the last paragraph of the instruction for 'Insertion circumjacent to the outer border' (*see p. 30*), C is as diagram 19 (*see p. 27*); D is the other diagonal but, because it extends out into the small square, follow the instruction for diagram 20 (*see p. 27*), to pass from one square to another; E is as B diagram 20. Complete the grid in this manner. Work the inner and outer arcs; work the woven shapes on to the extra grid bars to fill the distance between the two arcs.

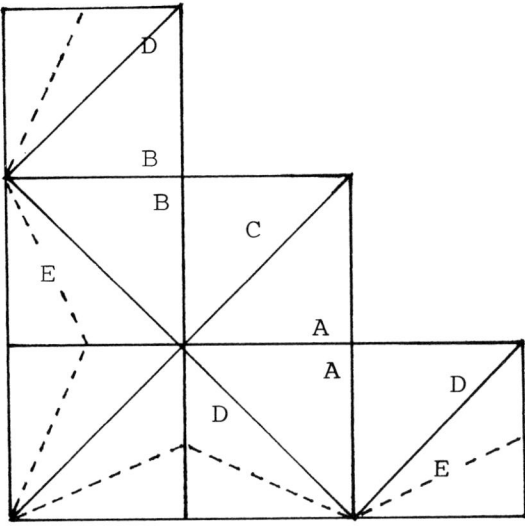

Diagram 54 *Grid for Pattern 49*

Figure 17 *Traycloth illustrating the use and siting of Pattern 49*

Pattern 50

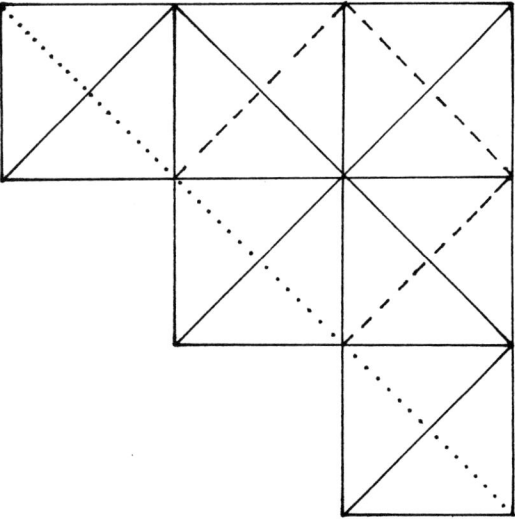

Diagram 55 *Grid for Pattern 50*

Lay and work the foundation grid as in the previous pattern as far as D. Complete as in diagram 55: work the diamond grid following the broken line; complete following the dotted line. The independent pyramids are worked as in Pattern 20 (*see p. 64*), the centre unit as in Pattern 10 (*see p. 61*).

The next two patterns are based on the window pattern foundation grid; the length can be increased by a unit repeat as for the plotting for an insertion (*see p. 29*). These patterns can be worked in sizes from 2½ in. to 3 in. (6.3 cm to 7.5 cm). All the square foundation grid is whip-stitched. Work all the short verticals before following diagram 26 (*see p. 35*) for the horizontal foundation bars. When a particular size or shape has to be repeated a number of times it is advisable to leave just one at foundation thread stage as a specimen, so enabling the worker to repeat a regular size.

Pattern 51

Work the diagonal grid as in diagram 27 (*see p. 36*); work the buttonhole-stitch circles encircling the eight-spoke junctions; the woven shapes radiate from this circle. The circles with picots are worked small and the stitches are closely packed so as to maintain a circle.

Pattern 52

When working the diagonal foundation bar observe the pattern, as a section of this bar, is worked in double buttonhole stitch and picots. The whole of the diamond foundation bar is worked in double buttonhole stitch and picots (refer to Pattern 48 *see p. 80*).

Increasing the length of the next two patterns is not as straightforward as in the previous two patterns. It can be done but care must be taken in the planning; it is advisable to draw it in full before working on the fabric. Again, these two patterns are based on the window pattern foundation grid, but neither has a diagonal nor a diamond grid. It will also be observed that the next two patterns are not based on a multiple of the depth, so the size of the individual square will be the unit, which, in this case, could be $\frac{1}{2}$ in. or $\frac{5}{8}$ in. (1.3 cm or 1.5 cm).

Pattern 53

Work the bold shapes, such as the shaped pyramids, first. Lay as many continuous foundation threads as possible.

Pattern 54

Again, position the shaped pyramid units first. It will be noted that one of the foundation bars forming the spokes to work the buttonhole-stitch and picot circle stretches from pyramid to pyramid only. Refer to diagram 56 to work the shape with the central H. Continue to buttonhole stitch three and a half sides. Repeat the linkage as in diagram 56, and complete the H with a one-thread bar connection or a three-thread bar and whip stitch. Complete the shape.

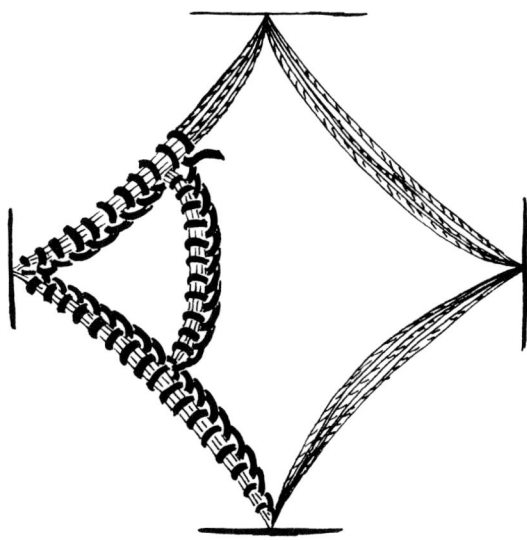

Diagram 56 *H-shape as in Pattern 54*

Figure 18 *Square mat illustrating Pattern 54 as an insertion circumjacent to the border*

The next two patterns can be repeated in units of two, and are most effective worked in unit sizes of $\frac{3}{4}$ in. or $\frac{7}{8}$ in. (2 cm or 2.2 cm). It will be noted that the basic foundation consists of one upright and one diagonal foundation bar; the latter needs care in positioning so that it passes through the corner correctly.

Figure 19 *Enlargement of Pattern 55 and figure 8, showing the buttonhole-stitched loop edging which overlaps an outside edge*

Pattern 55

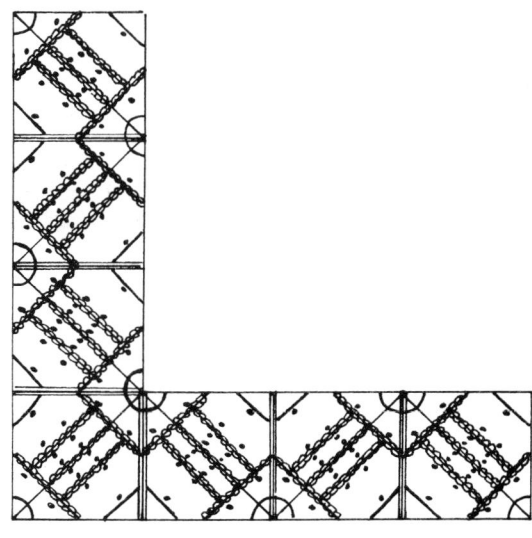

In this pattern the upright is woven as in diagram 21 (*see p. 28*). The double buttonhole-stitched inverted V on the inside circuit is worked first. As the inverted V bars are being worked from the outer circuit the double buttonhole stitch and picot bar linkages are worked. On the first and third linkage bars it is necessary to lay four foundation threads in order to continue working.

Figure 20 *Box top illustrating Pattern 56 used in conjunction with Pattern 23*

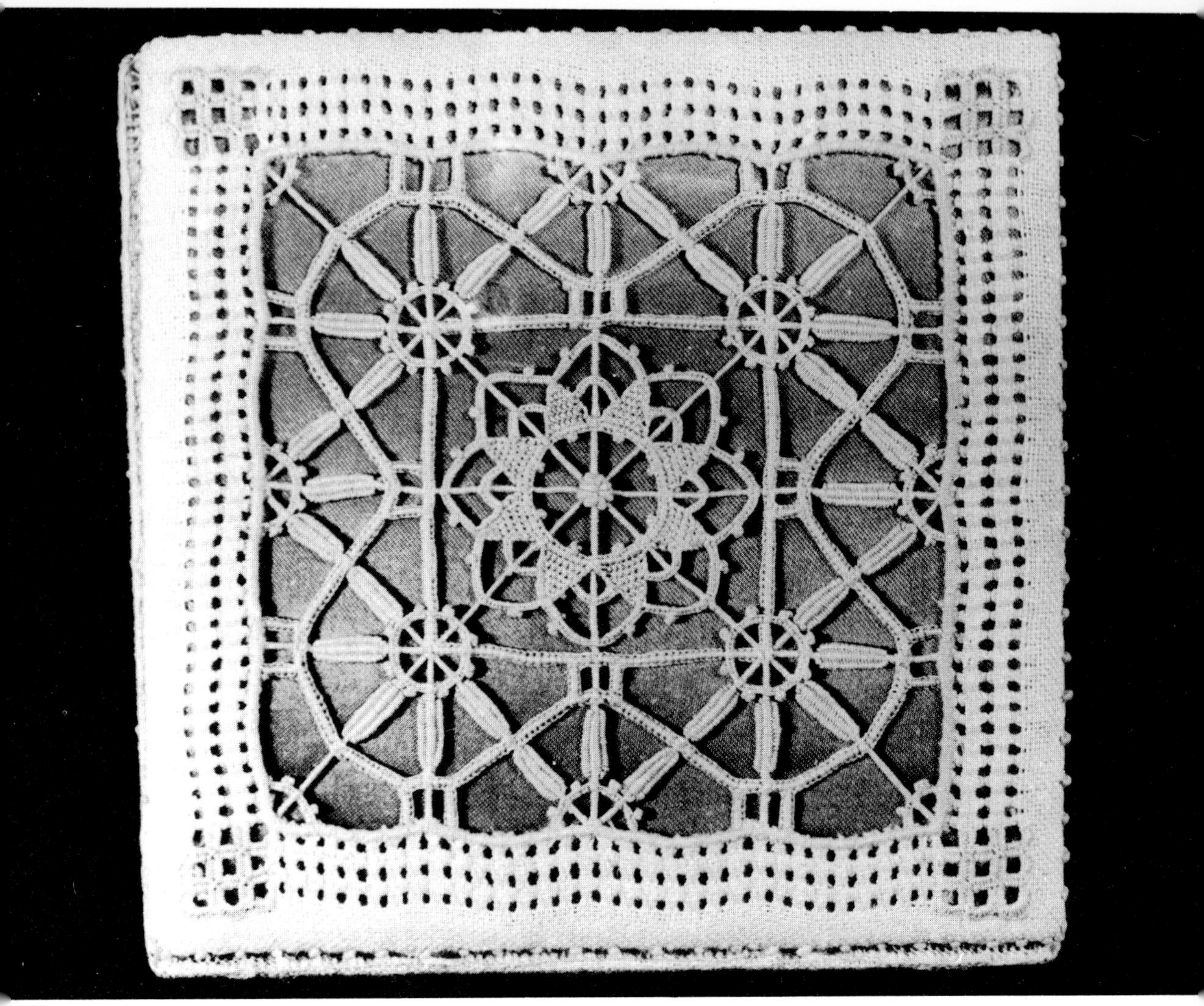

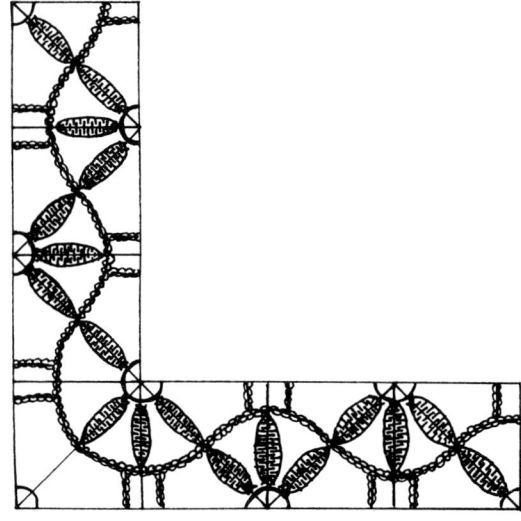

Pattern 56

After completing the foundation grid as above, the double buttonhole-stitch undulating bar is laid, passing through the diagonal bar at halfway, and creating a gentle curve as it passes each three-spoke junction. Picots can be added here if the worker so desires. Work the small whipped arc at the three-spoke junctions, working the woven shapes to radiate from the same point.

Pattern 57

This pattern can be worked into a $3\frac{1}{2}$ in. to $4\frac{1}{2}$ in. (9 cm to 11.5 cm) pattern area. Lay the foundation threads for the outer circle and work two rows of buttonhole stitch. Work the first circuit as usual. A foundation thread must be included in the second circuit. If on completion of the first circuit the remaining thread is long enough to reach a full circuit, then join a new thread and proceed. Otherwise, begin the new thread, leave an end long enough to use as a foundation thread and incorporate as required. On completion of the second circuit cut off the foundation thread and finish the working thread as usual. On the second circuit there will be no buttonhole stitch on top of the bar.

Then work the shapes of two rows of buttonhole stitch radiating from the circle which has just been completed. Begin by plotting one shape on to a square bar. Begin the thread on the circle. At A lay three foundation threads and buttonhole stitch, * continue to the next shape, lay one foundation thread and finish off thread. Re-join at A, lay two more foundation threads and buttonhole stitch *. Repeat from * to * as necessary. With a long length of thread begin on a foundation bar, leave a sufficiently long end to be incorporated as a foundation thread to reach full circuit and work through position A as in Pattern 4 at E (*see p. 58*).

Pyramids can now be worked. The shape inside the one just explained is buttonhole stitch with a picot towards the outer end. To work the undulating circuit it will be noted that the buttonhole stitch reverses. Begin the thread at B to lay the three threads for the outer shape; buttonhole stitch and picot; take the needle through the two rows of buttonhole stitch, lay three threads, work buttonhole stitch and finish the thread. Repeat as necessary. To work the outer linkage, begin the thread at the same side as B, lay three threads, buttonhole stitch, take a foundation thread back to the left, link into the outermost stitch where the foundation threads were attached and leave fairly loose to maintain the curve. At halfway attach to the padded roll with a one-thread or whipped bar.

When working on large areas it helps the control of the foundation bars if the centre junction is couched down to the leathercloth after being whipped, but release it before working the bullion knot centre.

Figure 21 *Box top using Pattern 57 with a covered bead in the centre*

Pattern 58

This pattern is based on the window pattern foundation grid and can be worked into an area from $3\frac{1}{2}$ in. to $4\frac{1}{2}$ in. (9 cm to 11.5 cm). The foundation threads are laid to work the pyramids in the corners in a continuous manner; the double buttonhole-stitching is not worked until all pyramids are complete.

For the centre unit the circle for the pyramids is laid and the pyramids worked; the innermost circle is then laid and worked in buttonhole stitch, one-thread bars and picots. The circular units inside the pyramid corner units are worked in a similar way; the outer is worked first and then the inner. If it turns out that the inner circle is to be very small, this is quite all right as the picots will form an attractive centre.

The outer units are two rows of buttonhole stitch with picots on the second row.

Pattern 59

This pattern can be worked into an area ranging from 4 in. to 5 in. (10 cm to 12.5 cm). The inner double circle unit is worked as for Pattern 3 (*see p. 57*), with a picot on the first and third one-thread bar. Lay the foundation threads as in Pattern 29 (*see p. 69*), which are whip-stitched except where the pyramids are to be worked.

The fourth circle out from the centre is buttonhole-stitched, with the buttonhole-stitched loop worked at the same time. * Buttonhole stitch one section less one stitch, lay three threads in the same manner as in diagram 52 (*see p. 60*) in between the first two buttonhole stitches, buttonhole stitch the loop, work one stitch on the circle and one buttonhole stitch on the bar*. Repeat from * to * as necessary. The outside units are worked in the same manner.

Pattern 60

This pattern has a foundation grid that divides the window pattern grid yet again; there are no diagonal foundation bars. Lay and work the diamond foundation bar. Lay the threads for the pyramids as continuously as possible; it will be noted that all pyramids can be worked from two rectangles. The foundation threads for the inner buttonhole-stitched and picoted shapes are laid as in diagram 56 (see p. 85). The buttonhole-stitch and picot circle need to be laid quite small so as to stand out as fairly bold units; there are two bullion knots laid obliquely over the centre junction of these units.

Edgings

Some form of edging is essential. No matter which form is chosen or how simple it is, the end result always justifies the time and effort involved. Even the simplest edging is guaranteed to enhance the work already done and is therefore, doubly satisfying.

Bullion knots

Single

The traditional edging is a single bullion knot worked over the outer edge of the fabric two threads in from the edge. The traditional spacing is $\frac{3}{8}$ in. (1 cm), but on small items it is preferable to work the knots approximately $\frac{1}{4}$ in. (6 mm) apart. Bullion knots can also be used as means of joining two edges together as in a pincushion, cushion or needlebook. The instruction for working bullion knots will be found in the text relating to diagram 45 (*see p. 45*).

Double

Bullion knots can be worked in pairs, side by side. These are worked as above but, after making the knot, bring the needle through to the right side slightly to the left of the first knot and work the second knot. Continue as above. Double bullion knots are most suitable where extra strength is needed, such as joining the edges of cushions, or, on larger articles, when a deep hem has been laid.

Treble

Treble bullion knots can be worked, usually on to large items such as tablecloths, when double bullions would not be bold enough to give a well-balanced effect. Treble bullion knots are worked as for the double knots, with a third knot over the fold of the previous two. After completing the second knot, take the needle in at the same place as the thread last came out and bring it out at the outer edge of the hem to the left of the two knots. Take the needle in at the other side of the two knots,

passing under the two and making contact with the fold of the fabric, and out where the thread came out. Make the bullion knot – this will lie across the fold of the two knots – and pass the thread through the hem to the next position, as before.

To finish a thread when making an edging, take the needle and thread through the hem (between the two layers of fabric) for approximately $\frac{1}{2}$ in. (1.3 cm) and, bringing the needle out on the wrong side, make a back stitch over one thread of fabric. Take the needle and thread through the hem as before without pulling, which would distort the fabric, and cut off the thread close to the fabric.

Buttonhole-stitched loops

These form a very versatile edging suitable to many situations. Buttonhole-stitched loops can either be worked singly or in various multiples, depending on the required effect. Multiple loops are usually applied to the edges of articles which will be surrounded by a margin of area in use, such as place mats and runners, etc. The size of this surface, will determine the space these multiple loops can occupy. Both single loops and multiple loops can be inter-spaced with bullion knots, worked as in diagram 45 (*see p. 45*). Picots can be worked on single loops or on the end loop of multiples.

An exception to the rule occurs here: it is necessary to lay four foundation threads so as to work the loops consecutively. These loops can be very shallow so that they lie very close to the edge of the fabric or they can stand off slightly, but if they are too deep there will be a tendency for them to twist and they will then not launder easily. These threads need to be laid slightly shallower than the required completed shape.

Singles

Begin the thread at the bottom left-hand cor-

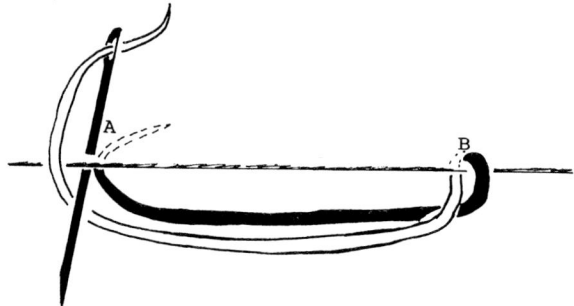

Diagram 57 *Four-thread loop, stage one*

ner of the article and work left to right, by taking the needle through between the two layers of fabric in the hem for approximately ½ in. (1.3 cm) and out on the outside edge of the article, as at A in diagram 57. Make a tiny stitch which will split the thread to secure it. Having decided the length of the loop (nine or ten threads distance between loops is average on the linen we normally use), take the needle in on the right side of the fabric at B and out on the underside approximately, one-thread deep into the fabric to form a loop stitch.

As the next corner of the article approaches the shapes need to be as even in length as possible, as with the bullion knots, so it will be necessary to plot the last 2 in. (5 cm) or so, so that the last repeat ends at the corner. A bullion knot can be worked diagonally over the corner.

Three-loop unit
A three-loop unit can either be worked as a continuous edging or interspaced with a bullion knot over the outer edge of the fabric.

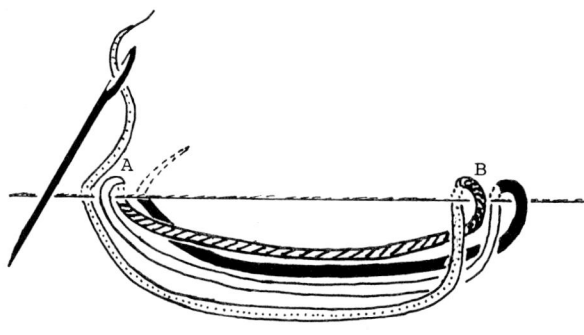

4th foundation thread

Diagram 58 *Four-thread loop, stage two*

Repeat, forming a loop stitch in reverse at A, then at B in diagram 58, then back to A, *but* bring the needle up from the underside to complete the fourth foundation thread. With the thread now on the right side of the work, work in buttonhole stitch over these four threads; a picot can be worked at halfway if desired.

Begin the thread as before at A in diagram 58, then to B, then to A then back to B, bringing the needle up from underneath here. The thread will now change direction without upsetting the formation of the previous loop. In the same manner, attach the thread at C in diagram 59, then to B, then back to C. Now lay the fourth foundation thread by bringing

94

Figure 22 *Enlargement of Pattern 54 and figure 18, showing the buttonhole-stitched loop edging overlapping the edge of a hem, here with a picot at halfway*

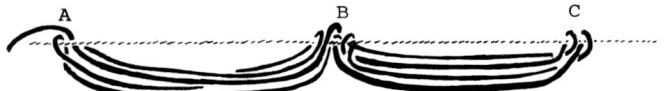

Diagram 59 *Four-thread base line loops*

the needle up from underneath at B, then from underneath at A. Work one and a half loops in buttonhole stitch and complete as in diagram 53 (*see p. 60*).

Multiple-loop unit

If a large multiple-loop unit is desired, it may be necessary to finish and restart a thread, as working the whole with one length of thread would present problems. Make sure that this happens at the stage of laying the foundation thread so that both ends of the threads can be worked in.

Loop which overlaps the outer edge of a hem

This edging gives a very pleasing result, especially when applied to a narrow hem, or where the surrounding area is going to be limited: picots can be added. It is a firm and stable edging and is useful to add to articles that will need to be laundered frequently (*see figures 19 and 22*).

This edging again is worked from left to right. Begin the thread in the same manner and in the same position as for the previous two edgings, but bring the needle out on the underside of the fabric two threads inside the edge of the fabric at A in diagram 60. Without the stitches showing through on to the right side, bring the thread closely around the outside edge of the hem and attach it at B, taking a good hold of a small amount of fabric two threads inside the edge of the fabric. Then back to A, back to B and back to A, making four foundation threads lying close to the edge of the fabric. Work in buttonhole stitch to B, making a picot at halfway if desired. Take the needle through to the underside which is the beginning of the next shape. Lay the next foundation threads between the underside of B and position C. The spacing of the loops is as before — approximately $\frac{1}{4}$ in. (6 mm) or nine or ten threads. The last repeat will complete as at A.

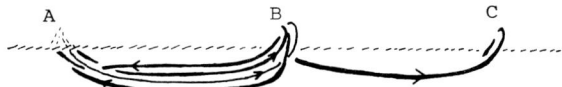

Diagram 60 *Laying threads for buttonhole-stitched loop which overlaps the outer edge of a hem*

96

Part III

ARTICLES

Ruskin lace will provide all those with the love of the needle with a channel for self expression and creativity, but deciding what to make can in itself present a problem. Sit down or wander around the home observing the blank spaces on the walls, the side tables, the dressing tables, particularly if they have plate glass protection; chairs that need protection to which some form of decoration can be added; the work box that has been waiting for a replacement pincushion or needlebook. Lampshades display this form of craft beautifully, although a lampshade is not recommended as a first article, and tablecloths and bedspreads can be long-term projects destined for family heirlooms.

Once the article has been chosen the decision for the depth of hem and pattern layout needs to be made. This will depend on the size of the article, its situation and, as always, personal choice. There are no laws, but it is perhaps worth stating that simplicity is the art of good design. Do your own thing. Take care to refer to the specific areas of your book for instruction.

It will be noted that most patterns can be worked over a size variation of approximately $\frac{1}{2}$ in. (1.2 cm) or more. It is advisable to work a few independent squares before venturing to the more complicated right angle of units or the multi-unit shape. The most beneficial size of square to work is approximately $2\frac{1}{4}$ in. (5.6 cm) as there is scope for practice in all stages, which will help to acquire a rhythm and regular tension.

Some of the following article sizes are designed specifically for the Glenshee Evenweave linen fabric we usually use which is 52 in. (132 cm) wide, so as to utilise the width to the best advantage with the minimum of wastage. In the main, the sizes of articles given are intended as suggestions. It is essential to remove the selvedges of the fabric; these will otherwise cause distortions in the hem after laundering. Draw a thread from the inside of

the selvedge then cut along the line of same. When purchasing linen of suitable weight for Ruskin work request that it be cut along a drawn-out thread.

Traycloth

The actual size is debatable as there are trays and trays, but a finished size of $10\frac{1}{2} \times 16\frac{1}{2}$ in. (27 × 42 cm) is average. The depth of the hem is also debatable; this can be $\frac{1}{4}$ in. (6 mm), $\frac{1}{2}$ in. (1.3 cm) or even deeper on the ends. The eventual size of the piece of fabric will be calculated according to the depth of hem which has been decided in 'To lay a hem' (*see* p. *17*).

A single or double row of four-sided stitch can be worked immediately inside the hem.

The permutations of design layout are endless and can be as simple or as complex as the worker desires. A few suggestions follow: (1) a square set diagonally in opposite corners; (2) a square in each corner, with a different pattern in each corner. These two layouts could be joined by a border of four-sided stitch linking the outer right angles of the squares. This link-up must be considered as the first square is being plotted. (3) An insertion at one or both ends of the cloth, depending on the length in proportion to the width. Here an insertion made up of an odd number of repeats is preferable, unless the worker intends to repeat the same pattern throughout the length of the insertion. (4) One larger square or other shape with three smaller squares in the other corners; these can be independent or linked with a border of four-sided stitch as in the first suggestion. Finally, any one of the various edgings can be added, as desired.

Place mats

A $\frac{1}{2}$ yd (46 cm) piece of Glenshee Evenweave linen 52 in. (152 cm) wide will make four place mats. The size of a place mat can be determined either by the size of the dining table and

Figure 23 *Place mats*

how many place settings the owner intends it to make, or the width of the fabric and how it can be best utilised. As a Glenshee width is 52 in. (132 cm), from a $\frac{1}{2}$ yd (46 cm) piece with selvedges removed the fabric can be equally divided into four mats approximately 18 × 12$\frac{3}{4}$ in. (46 × 30.5 cm) with no wastage. With a $\frac{1}{2}$ in. (1.3 cm) hem the completed article will be approximately 16$\frac{1}{2}$ × 11$\frac{1}{4}$ in. (41.8 × 28.6 cm) which will accommodate a place setting.

When considering the pattern layout avoid lace work in the upper right-hand corner which would make the positioning of a glass precarious and would also lose the focal interest. This is an article when the proverb 'simplicity is the art of good design' should be heeded. Natural fibre, natural colour on a natural wooden surface can present a stunning combination. Independent squares could be set on the diagonal, one at the bottom right

and another at the top left. These patterns could range from 1$\frac{1}{2}$ in. to 2$\frac{1}{4}$ in. inside area. An alternative could be an insertion, at one end only and preferably to lie on the left, made up of units ranging from 1 to 1$\frac{1}{2}$ in. (2.5 to 3.8 cm).

For the slightly more experienced worker a set of place mats could be made up from a variety of shapes or layout. For instance, two with diagonal squares, two with insertions, two with a right-angle unit in the top left-hand corner and two with a small multi-shape in the top left-hand corner. If a set of six were required, then make one of each of the above and divise two more different layouts. Allow the choice of edging to link the whole together as a set. Single bullion knots are usually sufficient, spaced at $\frac{3}{8}$ in. (1 cm) intervals.

Chairback covers

A $\frac{1}{2}$ yd (46 cm) piece of Glenshee Evenweave linen 52 in. (132 cm) wide will make a pair of average chairback covers. Size is debatable as there are many sizes of chairs, but a $\frac{1}{2}$ yd (46 cm) piece cut in two widthways of the fabric will give two pieces 26 × 18 in. (66 × 46 cm), and when the selvedges have been removed will result in a finished article 23 × 16$\frac{1}{2}$ in. (58.5 × 41.8 cm) which is roughly average. To arrive at this measurement, lay a $\frac{1}{2}$ in. (1.3 cm) hem on one end and the two long sides, with a 2 in. (5 cm) hem on the front drop end, as in diagram 2 (*see p. 18*) and diagram 61. Draw threads and work double four-sided stitch as in diagram 7, along all sides.

Chairback covers are a splendid way of showing off and enjoying Ruskin lace. Various pattern layouts are possible. Strong bold patterns are here worked to the best advantage, and can be in the form of independent squares, insertions or right-angle unit shapes. A few suggested pattern layouts are illustrated in diagram 62.

Runners

Experience reveals that of the many runners made no two of the same size can be recalled.

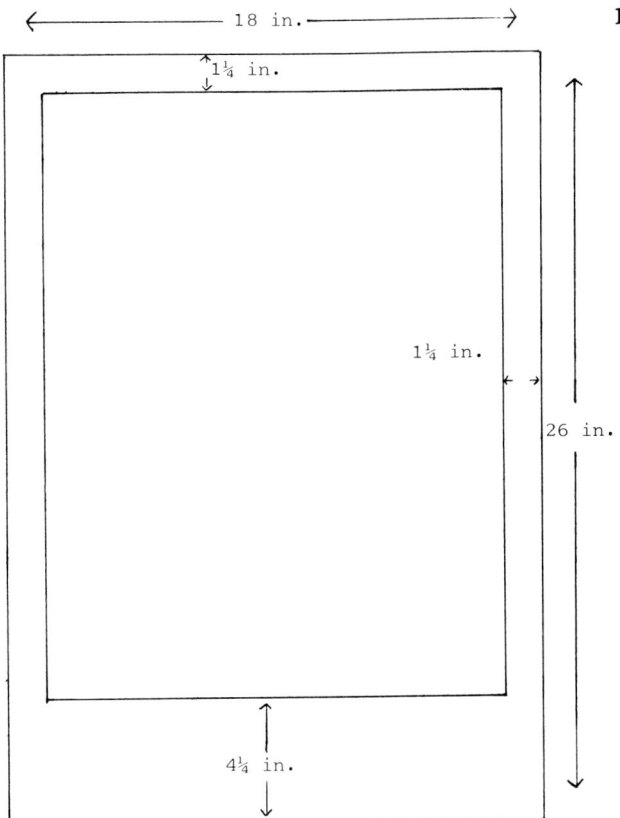

Diagram 61 *Laying a deeper hem on one end*

← 18 in. →

1¼ in.

1¼ in.

26 in.

4¼ in.

Diagram 62 *Suggestions for chairback pattern layout*

Figure 24 *Pincushions illustrating, from top left, Patterns 35 and 38, a variation of Pattern 24, and Pattern 32*

A runner is usually intended to enhance and not necessarily cover up, therefore it is advantageous to site it where there will be a good margin of surface all around. Think of the edging when deciding the margin; this is one situation where the three-loop unit can be worked to good advantage.

Pattern layout will be specifically determined by the siting of the objects which will also occupy the same piece of furniture.

If the runner is to be long and narrow, here is a situation where a deep hem on the ends and a narrow one on the sides will help to balance the proportions. If the runner is to be short and wide then the same depth of hem can be laid all round, from $\frac{1}{4}$ to 1 in. (6 mm to 2.5 cm). A single or double row of four-sided stitch can be worked.

Pattern areas can now be plotted avoiding areas to be otherwise occupied. In the case of a long, narrow runner, large square patterns will probably be the answer; if these are to be sited towards the ends, then it is possible to leave quite a margin at either end in order to attain a balance. It will help to cut squares of paper the size you have in mind and practise doodling before committing the scissors. Often on the short, wide runners an insertion plotted along each end is sufficient or one of the layouts suggested for the chairback cover.

Pincushion

There are pincushions of all shapes and sizes; the following measurements are just one suggestion.

Requirements

Two pieces of fabric, 5 × 5 in. (12.5 × 12.5 cm)
Two pieces of coloured lining fabric, 5 × 5 in. (12.5 × 12.5 cm)
Sheep wool, ideally, or synthetic filling.

Lay a $\frac{1}{4}$ in. (6 mm) hem on all sides of the two pieces to be used for Ruskin work (refer to instructions for diagram 1, 2 and 3 on pp. 17–19).

For the top piece, draw threads for a double row of four-sided stitch and on the other single four-sided stitch. Work as instructions for diagrams 4, 5, 5b, 6 and 7 (*see pp. 19–21*). On the top piece work woven corners as instructions for diagrams 8 and 9 (*see p. 21*).

The remaining inner area on the top piece will be pattern. Proceed as for the order of working to completion of the pattern chosen. When choosing a pattern for an article that is to be mounted at tension, make sure that the pattern has plenty of connections with the padded roll so as to avoid fluting of the padded roll, and that a bold, strong pattern is chosen. Complete, neaten corners on both pieces and press.

Make a pad the same size as the finished fabric pieces from the lining fabric by joining three sides. Pack well with the filling. If sheep wool is used, avoid washing if possible as the lanolin content will help prevent pins and needles rusting. Having said this, some types of fleece can have too much lanolin, but if it is not distinctly sticky to the touch it should be fine. If there is no alternative but to wash, then submerge the wool and leave to soak in a mild soapy solution, not detergent, until cold. Avoid excessive agitation as this will cause milling or shrinkage. Rinse well and spread out to dry naturally, teasing out well before stuffing the pad.

Along one side of the top piece, work single bullion knots as in diagram 45 (*see p. 46*), excluding the corners, approximately $\frac{1}{4}$ in. (6 mm) apart. Secure the two pieces of fabric to either side of the pad with pins and join the two pieces of fabric together along the other three sides with bullion knots. Take care to avoid making contact with the pad so that decades later it may be renewed without upsetting the stitchery. Make bullion knots over the corners at right-angles and diagonally – three in all; this protects the corners. With a separate thread, join the fourth side with a slip stitch.

Flat, sandwich pincushion

Requirements

Two pieces of fabric, 5 × 5 in. (12.5 × 12.5 cm)
Two pieces of coloured lining fabric, 5 × 5 in. (12.5 × 12.5 cm)
Two pieces of very thin card, $3\frac{1}{2}$ × $3\frac{1}{2}$ in. (9 × 9 cm)
Two pieces latex foam or wadding, $3\frac{1}{2}$ × $3\frac{1}{2}$ in. (9 × 9 cm)

Overcast the raw edges of the fabric. Plot a 2 in. (5 cm) pattern area square centrally on to one piece of fabric as in diagram 10 (*see p. 22*). Work the desired pattern to completion. Press. The other piece of fabric can be treated in the same way or work a square border of four-sided stitch only, approximately $1\frac{1}{2}$ in. (3.8 cm), as a light relief.

Secure the foam and wadding to the outer side of the pieces of thin card, a similar weight to that of good-quality greetings card. Cover the padded outer side of the card with lining fabric by lacing; do not glue. Cover the lined, padded, outer sides of the cards with the fabric, centralising the pattern, by lacing. Secure the two pieces together with bullion knots as in diagram 45 (*see p. 46*), $\frac{1}{4}$ in. (6 mm) apart, making two at right-angles and one diagonally at the corners.

The pins are then placed between the pieces of card. As there are four thicknesses of fabric between the cards the pins are quite secure.

Figure 25 *Flat pincushion*

Needle book

Requirements

Two pieces of fabric, 5 × 5 in. (12.5 × 12.5 cm)
Two pieces lining fabric, 4½ × 4½ in. (11.5 × 11.5 cm)
Two pieces Welsh flannel

Lay a ⅜ in. (1 cm) hem on all sides of both pieces, i.e. measure 1 in. (2.5 cm) from the outside edge of the fabric, pick up the next two inside threads and proceed as in the instruction for diagrams 1, 2 and 3 (*see pp. 17–19*).

For the top piece, draw threads for double four-sided stitch and work as instruction for diagram 7 (*see p. 21*). Work woven corners as in diagrams 8 and 9 (*see p. 21*). The whole of the inner area will be pattern. Proceed as order of working.

The under-piece can be worked as the top or just with a single border of four-sided stitch and three rows of single four-sided stitch worked vertically as on the reverse side of the pot-pourri sachet (*see figure 27, p. 107*), the centre row being longer than the other two. Two seven-stitch scallops will be needed to neaten the cut ends of thread. Complete both pieces and press.

To line both pieces allow single turning, overcast raw edges, fold under turning and tack into position so that the lining fabric comes to the outside edge of the hems. Secure the lining to the fabric with bullion knots on three sides of each piece.

To make up the book, ideally using Welsh Flannel, make two double pages. Cut along the grain of the fabric, fold the outer page in half and mark the fold. Secure with a running stitch the fold of the other piece slightly off centre so as to avoid excess bulk at the fold. Reduce the edges of all pages to the same overall size, ideally using pinking scissors. Secure the completed book to the under-side of the lined piece of fabric within the width of the hem of the unknotted side, so that the stitching will not show on the right side. Place the top piece of fabric so as to enclose the book and join the two pieces together with bullion knots along the fourth side.

Pot-pourri sachet

This is an article first designed by Mrs Raby which makes a popular and pleasing gift.

Requirements

A piece of fabric, 15 × 5 in. (38 × 12.5 cm)
A piece of coloured lining fabric, 12 × 4½ in. (30.5 × 12 cm)

A 1 in. (2.5 cm) hem is laid at each end and a ¼ in. (6 mm) hem on the long sides. Begin plotting at one end of the fabric, as in diagram 63 where a single line represents two drawn-out threads. Measure 2¼ in. (5.6 cm) from the outside edge at one end of the fabric and pick up the next two innermost threads on the pin. Measure ⅝ in. (1.5 cm) from the outside edge on both sides and pick up the next two threads well away from the point where the cut threads will meet at the junction of the two corners. Cut the three pairs of picked-up threads and draw back towards the end of fabric, forming two right angles.

Fold the length of fabric in half along the grain of one thread and run a marker thread in this position. Measure ¼ in. (6 mm) from the fold, pick up two threads on side A, cut these

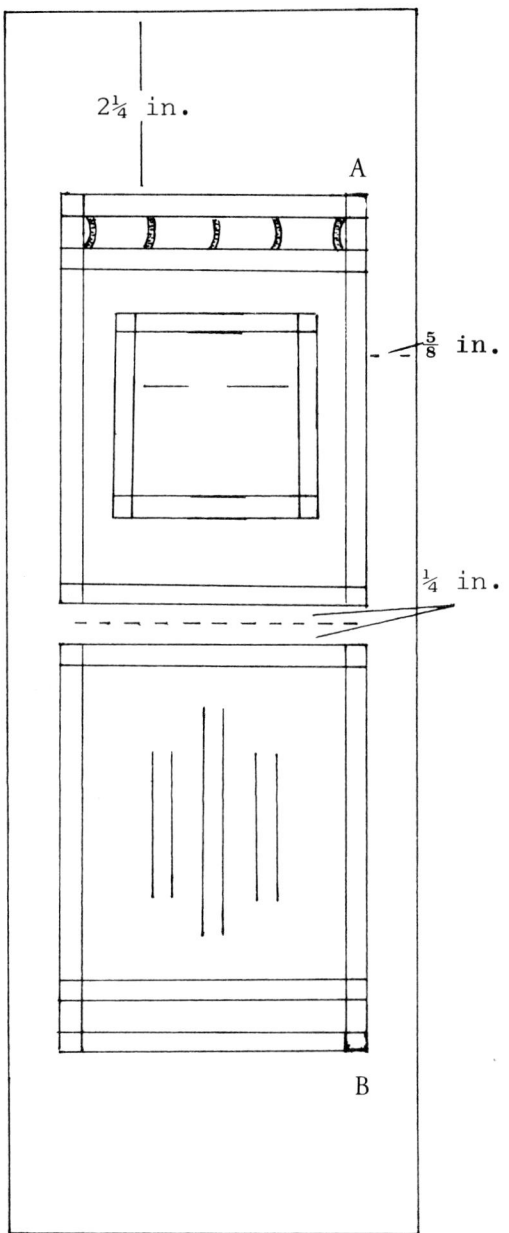

2¼ in.

A

$\frac{5}{8}$ in.

$\frac{1}{4}$ in.

B

Diagram 63 *Pot-pourri sachet layout*

two threads and draw back to form a rectangle with the other cut threads.

To draw threads for side B, measure $\frac{1}{4}$ in. (6 mm) from the fold, pick up two threads and trace the two pairs of threads already cut on side A through the margin at the fold; these form the sides of B. Cut these three pairs of threads and draw back to form two right-

angles. Measure 2¼ in. (5.6 cm) from the end, pick up two threads, cut these and draw back to complete the other rectangle.

Fold the hems as in diagram 2 (*see p. 18*), with long sides first, to form a $\frac{1}{4}$ in. (6 mm) hem. Cut away excess bulk as in diagram 2 (*see p. 18*), but in the case of a $\frac{1}{4}$ in. (6 mm) hem only the depth of the first turning is removed. Fold the ends to form a 1 in. (2.5 cm) hem. Tack and slip stitch as in diagram 3 (*see p. 19*).

Complete the thread-drawing for the four-sided stitch border on both rectangles as in diagram 4 (*see p. 19*). Leave a margin of 12 threads from each end immediately inside the four-sided stitch border, pick up the next two threads, leave four, pick up two and cut and draw back to the outside of the border on the sides, forming an isolated block of four threads as at a right angle or corner. Woven loops will be worked across this margin later to take a draw cord.

Plot a square for a pattern as suggested in diagram 10 (*see p. 22*); this can be repeated on side B if desired, or three columns of four-sided stitch as illustrated in figure 27 (*see p. 107*). Work four-sided stitch borders and pattern as per order of working.

Neaten all cut ends of threads. Where two rows of four-sided stitch borders interlock there are two pairs of threads to neaten on the straight. Work two seven-stitch shapes as in diagrams 47 and 48 (*see p. 47*). Press.

Woven bars span the 12-thread margin. Lay six threads formed by three circuits, as in diagram 41 (*see p. 44*), securing the threads into the margin threads one and 12. Work as in diagram 21 (*see p. 28*). Start and finish working threads by running through the crosses on the under-side of the four-sided stitch. Place five woven bars equally spaced on each side of the sachet, one inside each four-sided stitch border at the hems, one centrally and one in each quarter.

The lining is made of a colour and type of the worker's choice, to enclose the full width and the four-sided stitch borders at each end. Allow turnings: these will probably need to be overcast. Fold turnings to the under-side and tack into position as in diagram 64. Work bullion knots along the ends beginning and

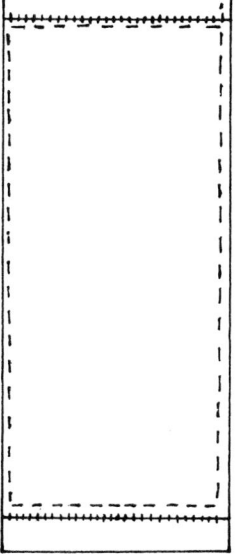

Figure 26 *Pot-pourri sachet using linen spun and woven by the author*

ending a ¼ in. (6 mm) from the sides, as in diagram 64, making the knots approximately ¼ in. (6 mm) apart.

Fold in half and join the sides with bullion knots as in diagram 45 (*see p. 46*). Begin with two bullion knots close together at the bulk of the 1 in. (2.5 cm) hem and the lining, and work towards the fold making the knots ¼ in. (6 mm) apart. Re-start at the same place on the other side and repeat. Then work bullion knots at the same spacing around each open end.

There are various methods of making twisted cords, but the method used here is as follows.

Use the same thread as that used in the needlepoint and three pencils or similar objects. Estimate three times the finished length and as many thicknesses as required, but six to

Diagram 64
Lining pot-pourri sachet

106

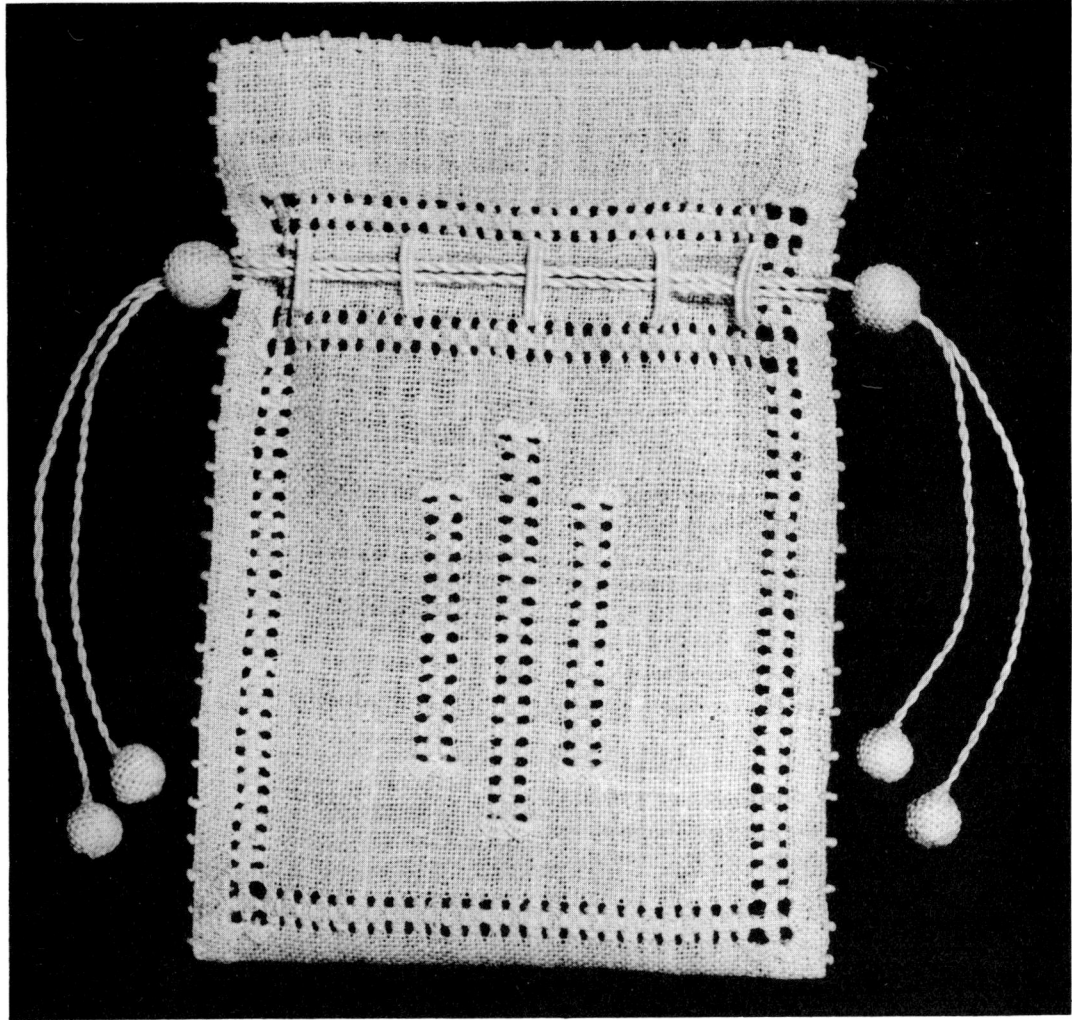

Figure 27 *Pot-pourri sachet showing the reverse side*

eight are average. Threads with a softer twist will tend to make a softer cord, so adjustments may need to be made. Make a loop at each end to take a pencil. If you can enlist the help of an assistant, take an end each and twist in the same direction. If not, you will need to secure one end and the performance takes twice as long. Twist until very hard, taking note of the direction of twisting. With care, fold in half, placing the third pencil in the fold. Proceed to twist in the opposite direction until the cord is again quite hard. Remove the third pencil. When tension is released some twist will

unwind but a good depth of twist will be maintained; it will be noticed that when cut the cord does not easily untwist as with a single twisted cord.

Cut two pieces of cord approximately 20 in. (51 cm) long. Thread each piece through the full circuit of woven bars in both directions and knot the ends together, or finish as desired. In figure 27 it will be noted that wooden beads have been threaded on to the cord enclosed in a continuous circuit of buttonhole stitch. To thread the beads on to the cord: at the third pencil end all the threads are doubled; pass a length of fine thread through all the loops and then thread a needle with both ends of the same thread. Before cutting the cord thread one small bead and one large bead on to the far end of the cord (loosely knot the end of the cord to contain the beads), thread the cord through the woven loops for one full circuit, pass the cord through the large bead again and thread on another small bead. Cut the cord as required. On to the remaining length, thread one small bead and one large bead, thread the cord through the woven loops in the reverse direction to the first circuit, thread through the large bead again and add the last small bead.

To work over the beads the working thread must be long enough to complete the buttonhole stitch and provide a foundation thread. When a bead needs to be attached to the end of the cord untwist approximately 1 in. (2.5 cm) of cord, spread out the ends and fold back over the bead. Thread a Sharps needle and hold in the right hand. With the right hand make two anticlockwise circuits of the cord just above the bead to control and enclose the loose ends, as in diagram 65. Leave a long end of thread to be incorporated as a foundation thread later. Work a circuit of buttonhole stitch over the two anticlockwise threads. If these threads become loosened in so doing, draw on the free end to close. Now incorpor-

Diagram 65 *Covering a bead*

ate the free end and continue in detached buttonhole stitch. To increase, work two stitches into one in-between space as necessary; decrease by missing an in-between space. To finish the thread, pass the needle through the bead, through the cord and back through the bead, make a contact with the last circuit and repeat. Tie the needle thread and foundation thread together, thread the needle with the foundation thread and pass through the bead as above. Cut off both threads and excess cord threads.

For the larger beads that need to slide freely on the cord, work as above, but there will be no ends to enclose. To finish off threads do not pass through the bead but through the mass of buttonhole-stitching, making a back stitch over a loop without it showing. Repeat, unthread the needle and treat the foundation thread in the same way.

Bag

The base is an octagon based on a 10 in. (25 cm) diameter circle. The measurement of the sides of the octagon determines the finished width of the panels; the finished height is approximately $10\frac{1}{4}$ in (25.6 cm). This bag could be used as a work bag as originally intended but, of course, it could have other uses.

Requirements
Fabric, 12 × 52 in. (30.5 × 132 cm)
Coloured lining fabric 27 × 45 in. (68.5 × 115 cm)
2 mm hardboard or other suitable material, 12 × 24 in. (30.5 × 61 cm)
1 mm card, 12×12 in. (30.5x30.5 cm)
4 mm latex foam, 24x24 in. (61x61 cm)

To make the panels cut eight pieces from the fabric, each measuring $4\frac{3}{4}$ × 12 in. (12 × 30.5 cm). Plot as in diagram 66, where a single line represents two drawn-out threads. Lay a $\frac{1}{4}$ in. (6 mm) hem on three sides and a 1 in. (2.5 cm) hem on the top. Tack and slip stitch. Complete the thread-drawing for single four-sided stitch border. From the top border count 12 threads immediately inside and draw

Figure 28 *Associated Country Women of the World Handicraft Competition, third prize in 1977; designed and worked by the author*

threads for another border. At the base end draw threads for the fourth side of a square. The measurements of the area between the side borders determines the size of the square. On four of the panels the whole of this area is pattern. Work all four-sided stitch *. Work the pattern area following the order of working and the pattern chosen. On the other four panels, work as above to *, then plot a smaller square inside the square already plotted by leaving a margin of eight threads on all sides. Work patterns from the $1\frac{1}{2}$ in. (3.8 cm) group. Press. Work woven bars exactly as for the pot-pourri sachet (*see p. 105*).

From the 2 mm hardboard cut the base and eight squares the width of the panels. Chamfer the inside edges of the base and three inside edges of the squares (male assistance may need to be enlisted here). From the 1 mm card cut a base lining fractionally smaller than the hardboard base. Secure 4 mm latex foam to the outside of the base and the inside of the base lining card, and both sides of the squares. Use the minimum of glue possible and avoid glue coming in to contact with edges where stitching has to be worked later.

Cover the outside of the base with fabric, secure with glue or lacing and cut away excess

Diagram 66 *Bag panel*

bulk where the turned-under fabric overlaps. Cover the inside of the base lining with lining fabric in the same way. Secure base and base lining together.

If it is intended to include some pockets to the inside of the bag, they should be secured to the lining fabric pieces before the squares are covered. When cutting out the lining fabric pieces to cover the squares, allow a 1 in (2.5 cm) turning all around. Secure the lining fabric to the inside area of the square; as both sides of the square are padded, lacing would be preferable to glue. Join the squares together with ladder stitch, keeping all the unchamfered edges in the same position to become the top, unattached, edge later. Take care in positioning the pockets – they are not too functional upside down! Secure the joined squares to the base without the stitches making contact with the extreme outer edge of the base.

Join the long sides of the panels together with bullion knots, alternating the large patterned panels with the small patterned panels. Leaving the top ends open, as in the potpourri sachet (*see p. 106*) and work bullion knots around the open ends.

Make a twisted cord, as for the pot-pourri sachet, long enough to form two generous circuits plus 16 in. (40.5 cm) for finishes as in figure 28.

Lampshades

The traditions of Ruskin work restrict the shape of a lampshade to that of a drum. As drum-shape lampshade frames are not manufactured, a top and bottom loose ring is used with a self-adhesive card stiffening material to maintain a firm shape. The self-adhesive card has a peel-off backing which exposes a tacky surface to which a coloured lining fabric can be adhered. The lace-worked fabric is then mounted on to it, producing a very attactive way of displaying Ruskin work. Because each frame is made up by the worker, she can choose the height of the shade. The loose rings are obtainable in diameter sizes ranging from 6

Figure 29 *Lampshade illustrating a random pattern layout*

to 18 in. (15 to 46 cm), the usual being 7, 8 or 9 in. (18, 20.5 or 23 cm).

Requirements
One plain ring and one ring with a utility or gimbal fitting
Self-adhesive card of height and circumference required
Coloured lining fabric to cover the above plus sufficient to cut bias strips
Fabric, the height plus hem allowances × the circumference, plus 3 in. (7.5 cm)
$\frac{1}{4}$ in. (6 mm) straight tape to bind the rings

Lay a $\frac{1}{2}$ in. (1.3 cm) hem on both long sides and one end, as in diagram 67. Place a tack line to show the expected circumference and one centrally horizontal; this will help if any pattern unit needs to be plotted from the centre of the height.

The pattern layout can be random or very organised. As the layout can not be viewed as a whole when the lampshade is completed it is not, therefore, necessary to balance it. Avoid pattern areas being sited so that two come together when the ends are eventually joined. If patterns are plotted in the top corner at one end, then plot the last pattern in the lower corner at the other end. The layout does need to be fairly concentrated as, when mounted, the size of the unworked areas becomes exaggerated. Squares can be linked and set obliquely; these squares do not need to be all the same size. Insertions can be included, though not longer than three units. These are usually placed horizontally as odd insertions placed vertically tend to break the continuity of the layout. A layout using vertical insertions only, however, is very pleasing; the number of units high will be determined by the plotting height available which, in turn, will determine the number of insertions required to fill the circumference.

Pattern areas can be plotted from a margin of $\frac{1}{2}$ in. (1.3 cm) at the hemmed end to within $\frac{1}{2}$ in. (1.3 cm) of the tack line registering the net circumference. Complete all the lace work.

To make up the shade, paint the rings (not the fitting bar) with any type of paint – even nail varnish is adequate. Bind the rings with

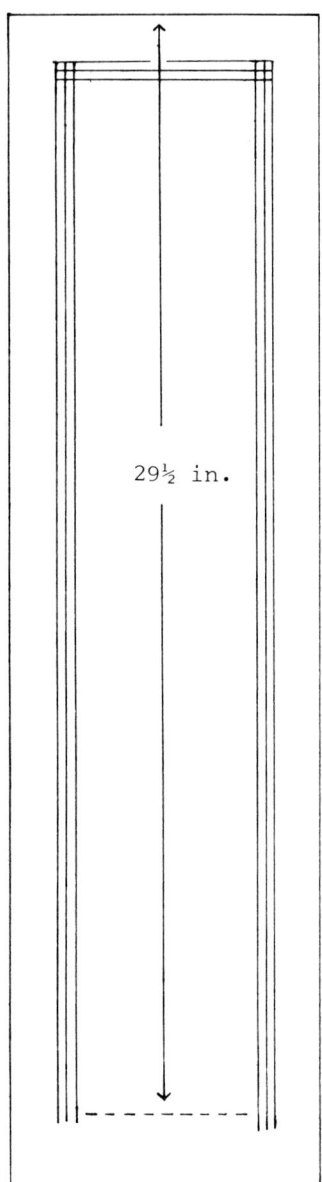

$29\frac{1}{2}$ in.

Diagram 67 *Hems for lampshade fabric*

Figure 30 *Lampshade illustrating an organised pattern layout*

the $\frac{1}{4}$ in. (6 mm) straight tape with a generous overlap. Bind the rings with $1\frac{1}{4}$ in. (3.2 cm) wide bias strips cut from the coloured lining fabric. Make any joins needed on the bias, and use a separate length for each ring. Stretch out the bias under an iron set at a heat suitable for that type of fabric – this will reduce the width

considerably – and press a narrow turning on one long side of the strips. Place the strip around the ring horizontally, tucking the raw edge under the folded one; if it is too bulky then reduce the width of the strip. Using thread to match that of the coloured lining, secure with over-sewing along the outer circumfer-

112

ence of the ring, so that these stitches will be covered when the stiffening is attached.

Measure the depth of the lace-worked fabric at a point where the pattern is most concentrated; this determines the depth of the self-adhesive card. Cut the self-adhesive card, depth × net circumference plus 2 in. (5 cm). Using spring-type clothes pegs, peg the self-adhesive card to the covered rings, allowing an overlap of $\frac{1}{2}$ in. (1.3 cm). Cut off the excess. Cut the lining fabric to this size, plus at least $\frac{1}{4}$ in. (6 mm) all round – more can be left then reduced later. Roll the lining fabric on to a card roller (kitchen tissue or tin foil), wrong side outer-most. The self-adhesive card tends to be slightly unwieldy. Place one end on to a table or working surface, tacky side upper-most, with the surplus hung over the edge, and control it by leaning against it. Peel off approximately 4 in. (10 cm) of the backing and place the lining fabric on to it, registering it straight with equal allowance at the end and both sides. Do not press together. Peel off and unroll to the other end, a few inches at a time. Reduce allowances to $\frac{1}{4}$ in. (6 mm) and ease the lining off the tacky surface at the edges to fold under the allowance. The lining fabric can come to the outside edge on the long sides but *not* at the ends; leave an $\frac{1}{8}$ in. (3 mm) margin of tacky surface showing here.

Secure the lined self-adhesive card to the rings, lining outermost with spring pegs. Using stab stitch attach the self-adhesive card to the rings, recessing the rings approximately $\frac{1}{8}$ in. (3 mm)–no more. Begin the thread with a knot. To work from right to left, * pass the needle on the slant through the self-adhesive card in a forward-moving direction into the ring covering, pass back through the ring covering in the same place as the needle came out and through the self-adhesive card again on a forward-moving slant. Leave approximately $\frac{3}{8}$ in. (1 cm) and repeat from * to within $2\frac{1}{2}$ in. (6.3 cm) of the end. Secure the thread. Turn the shade upside down, begin the thread $2\frac{1}{2}$ in. (6.3 cm) from the end and proceed from *. Press worked fabric. ** Whilst still damp, pin, so that the tacked circumference line is on the end of the $2\frac{1}{2}$ in. (6.3 cm) flap, into the lining fabric only. With pin heads towards the length of fabric, wrap the fabric around the shade. If the hemmed end will meet the tack

line with a little stretching, then all is well; if not, note the distance by which it falls short, re-set a tack line in this position and place this in the same position as above. The four-sided stitch border may need to be extended. Remove the pins. Work bullion knots along the short hemmed end, approximately $\frac{1}{4}$ in. (6 mm) apart, leaving the corners free. If the linen has dried out or become crushed then re-press and re-attach as from **. Stab stitch the lined self-adhesive card and the worked fabric together as in diagram 68, $\frac{1}{4}$ in. (6 mm) in from the end of the self-adhesive card and $\frac{3}{8}$ in. (1 cm) apart. Because there is a $\frac{1}{2}$ in. (1.3 cm) overlap this stitching should not be visible from the inside of the completed shade. Reduce the surplus outer fabric to $\frac{1}{4}$ in. (6 mm) from the stab stitch and oversew the raw edge.

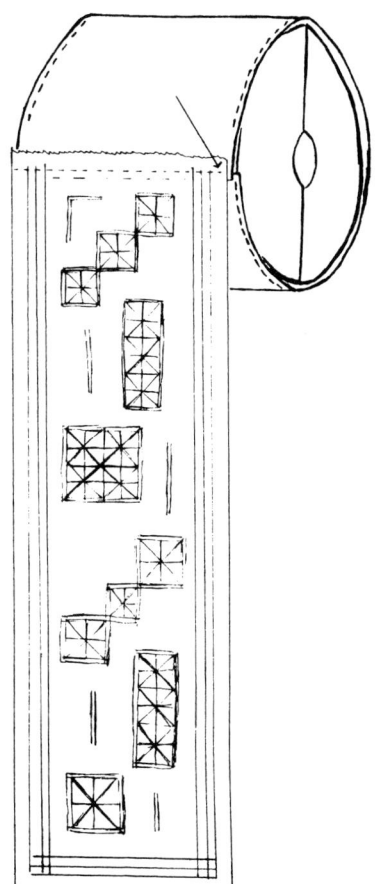

Diagram 68 *Attaching lampshade fabric to self-adhesive card*

Wrap the fabric around the shade and pin the hemmed end to reach the tack line. The pinning may need to be repeated a few times in order to make the end reach the desired position, so pin, then begin at one end and persuade it to reach a little further across, repeating if necessary. Remove the tack line. Using self thread, ladder stitch the two ends together.

Secure the top and bottom edges together with bullion knots, two threads deep into the fabric and over the top of the self-adhesive card, taking a good hold of the latter. The bullion knots will need quite a few more twists than usual, especially when passing over where the two ends meet. Put as many twists on the needle as is necessary to form the length the knot has to reach. When knotting the second circumference the fabric may need stretching to fit. This will ensure the fabric is evenly taut over the shade.

Wallhangings

These are a versatile use for Ruskin work. A wallhanging will be free-mounted and will, therefore, need a hem lying on all sides, probably a deeper hem on the lower end. As there will be a four-sided stitch border, some of the patterns can be linked into it. Avoid placing a central pattern shape or any borders that occur on the same parallel, otherwise the eye will 'home in' on the centre pattern or connect the borders so marring the visual pleasure. Stagger or interlock the pattern areas as much as possible, as in the Victoria and Albert Museum sampler (*see the frontispiece*) or figure 31 on p. 115 of the small wallhanging. Patterns plotted on the oblique will help the eye to travel around the article. If the article is to be long and narrow avoid insertion shapes set on the horizontal as this could interfere with the visual flow; these shapes can be equally disadvantageous set vertically as this will exaggerate the narrowness. When designing a complex layout it is perferable to make an actual size plan, using a plain paper background and cutting shapes of the lace-work area sizes from either a contrast paper or newsprint. When securing these shapes to the plan allow a $\frac{1}{4}$ in. (6 mm) all around to accommodate the four-sided stitch border. Begin the thread-drawing for the pattern areas that will be most dominant, after which it may be necessary to make amendments to the plan in order to practise the above suggestions.

The worked fabric will then need to be mounted on to a backcloth; this can be of felt, leathercloth or suede and is usually of a contrasting colour. The mount will need to be stiffened along the top and a means of hanging, probably with a cord, attached. The mount will be larger than the worked fabric, as in figure 31.

Pictures

If the picture is to be glazed, the worked fabric will be laced on to a rigid mount and will, therefore, need an all round allowance of approximately 3 in. (7.5 cm). As there will be no hems, there is no need for a continuous four-sided stitch border, which makes mounting the fabric considerably easier. (If there was a continuous border the lacing would need to be extremely accurate as any variation of tension would be very obvious.) Place a tack line at the position immediately inside the frame. The mount will eventually be this size, plus the rebate depth on the frame. A coloured lining fabric will also need to be laced on to the mount.

When planning the layout, avoid any two pattern shapes on the same side occurring at the same margin from the tack line. The planning suggestions for the wallhanging also apply here.

If the fabric is to be mounted close to the glass, bullion knot centres to any pattern are to be avoided; if a slight recess between the glass and the mount can be achieved then bullion knots can be worked to advantage, as these do add depth and texture to a pattern.

Figure 31 *Small wall hanging illustrating one of the many permutations of pattern layout. This one is mounted on to felt, as the overall linen size is only $16\frac{1}{2} \times 11\frac{1}{2}$ in. (41.8×29.3 cm).*

Conclusion

Heaven preserve me from a wife
with fancy work run wild,
with hands which never do aught else
for husband or for child.
Our clothes are torn
our bills unpaid
our house is in disorder,
and all because my lady wife
has taken to embroider.

A verse from the 'Husband's Complaint' (slightly changed), from *A History of Needle-making*, by M. T. Morral, 1852. If this verse can be read without producing a smile then this book has not been enjoyed as intended.

Figure 32 *Book back or cover: a suggestion for pattern layout which could be used in many other ways and with many other types of backings*

List of Suppliers

Wholesale - Linen

LanScot - Textile Mfg. Limited
Units 1 & 2
Lanscot House
Woodend Business Centre
Cowdenbeath
Fife KY4 8HG
Tel: (01383) 515132/515186
Fax: (01383) 513571

Retail - Linen

Russells Needlework
34 Castle Street
Carlisle
Cumbria CA3 8TP
Tel: (01228) 43330

Camden Needlecraft
Chipping Camden
Glos. GL55 6AG
Tel: (01386) 840 583

Y Needlecraft
No. 2 Royal Oak Place
Matlock Street
Bakewell
Derbyshire DE45 1HD
Tel: (01629) 815 198

The Embroidery Shop
51 William Street
Edinburgh EH3 7LW

The Craft House
20 Bar Street
Scarborough YO11 2HT

Nancy's Embroidery Shop
273 Tinakori Road
P.O.Box 245
Wellington
New Zealand
Tel: (04) 473 4047

E. M. Colgrave
80 Dewar Terrace
Sherwood
QLD 4075
Australia

Cotton Crafts
462 Fullarton Road
Myrtle Bank
Adelaide
Australia

Christine Riley
53 Barclay Street
Stonehaven
Tayside
Scotland

The Sewing Basket
55 Fort Street
Ayr
Strathclyde
Scotland

Retail - Thread

Barleycroft Lace Supplies
(Mrs G. Hare)
Honeypuddle
13 Barleycroft
Stevenage
Herts., SG2 9NP

Mrs J. R. Finlay
Kastania
Kingston Road
Shalbourne
Marlborough
Wilts., SN8 3QD

J & J Ford
October Hill
Upper Way
Upper Longdon
Rugeley
Staffs., WS15 1QB

Central Scotland Lace Supplies
3 Strude Howe
ALVA
Clackmannanshire
Scotland FK12 5JU

Jo Firth
58 Kent Crescent
Lowtown
Pudsey
West Yorkshire, LS28 9EB

Heathside Crafts
149 West Heath Road
Farnborough
Hants., GU14 8PL

Hill Crafts
Wysing House
Smelthouses
Summerbridge
Harrogate
N. Yorks., HG3 4DL

D. J. Hornsby
25 Manwood Avenue
Canterbury
Kent, CT2 7AH

The Lace Place
(Mrs Janis Savage)
P.O. Box 2126
Honeydew 2040
South Africa

Mainly Lace
Moulsham Mill
Parkway
Chelmsford
Essex CM2 7PX

Jane & Tony Martin
Broomfield Bobbins
41 Broomfield Road
Henfield
W. Sussex, BN5 9UD

Tim Parker
124 Corhampton Road
Boscombe East
Bournemouth
Dorset, BH6 5NZ

Heronsmead Crafts
Heronsmead
Bridgwater Road
Lympsham
Somerset, BS24 0BP

Hobbycraft
7 Church Street
Huntly
Aberdeenshire AB54 5DG

Gaynor Kelly
Gavand Enterprises
267 Luton Road
Dunstable, Beds., LU5 4LR

Larkholme Lace
37 Larkholme Parade
Fleetwood, Lancs., FY7 8LL

Makit Direct Ltd
The Old Post Office
101 High Street
Offord D'Arcy
Huntingdon
Cambs., PE18 9RH

Josie Sear
Lacecraft Supplies
8 Hill View
Sherington
Bucks., MK16 9NJ

Sebalace
Waterloo Mill
Howden Road
Silsden
Keighley
W. Yorks., BD20 0HA

Stitches & Lace
Alby Craft Centre
Cromer Road
Alby
Norwich
Norfolk, NR11 7QE

Mrs Lynn Turner
Church Meadow Crafts
15 Carisbrook Drive
Winsford
Cheshire
CW7 1LN

West End Lace Supplies
Orchid Cottage
Drury Lane
Mortimer Common
Reading, RG7 2JN

Arthur Sells
Lane Cove
49 Pedley Lane
Clifton
Shefford
Beds.

Trician Crafts
27 Ashtree Road
Cosby
Leicester
LE9 5UA

Mrs V. S. Walton
Biggins Bobbins
1 Archery Close,
Cliffe Woods
Rochester
Kent, ME3 8HN

Lampshade Materials

Fred Aldous
Lever Street
Manchester M60 1UX
Tel: (0161) 236 2477

Flannel

Trefriw Woollen Mills Ltd
Trefriw
Gwynedd
North Wales LL27 0NQ

Bibliography

Rev. H. D. Rawnsley, *Ruskin and the English Lakes*, J. MacLehose and sons.

Frederick A. Benjamin, *The Ruskin Linen Industry of Keswick*, Micheal Moon.

H. H. Warner, *Songs of the Spindle and Legends of the Loom*, N. J. Powell and Co.

Marguerite Blake, *Revival of Spinning and Weaving in Langdale*

Patricia Baines, *Spinning Wheels, Spinners and Spinning*, B. T. Batsford Ltd.

D.M.C. Needlemade Laces, Th. de Dillmont.

Jane Lemon *Embroidered Boxes*, Faber and Faber.

Index